CW00501977

INSIDE BRITISH PRISONS

By

Jack Jones

An original work first published January 2020
by
Aylen Useful Information Publishing

CONTENTS

INTRODUCTION

I decided to write this book because if you've never had the misfortune to have been in a British prison then you don't have an accurate idea of what it's like to be 'inside' and while I can't describe accurately what it's like to be 'inside' serving a sentence, I have hopefully created a book that contains information that may be useful for you, a relative or a friend and it is my hope this will make the prison process a little smoother for all involved by removing some of the 'mystery'.

Of course, you may have bought this book just to be a well informed person or to be nosy and I don't blame you, in fact, had this book existed when I first entered the Prison Service then I'd have been a lot better prepared and would have gladly paid five times the price you paid!

TV series like Porridge, Orange Is The New Black or Prison Break and films like Scum, Starred Up or The Shawshank Redemption don't show the reality of prison life in the UK, partly because they're dramas, partly because they're out of date and the ones based on American prisons thankfully have little in common with the British reality. Even the most recent reality based attempts such as Inside Prison and Ross Kemp's Welcome to HMP Belmarsh give you only the briefest edited idea of some aspects of prison life, this book will hopefully fill in the blanks and provide a comprehensive view of life behind bars.

For many people the idea of spending time in prison does not cross their minds, being generally law abiding individuals but it's actually a lot easier than you might think to find yourself a guest of Her Majesty.

Have you ever driven a little too fast?

Maybe had 2 beers or glasses of wine before driving a mile or two down the road?

Made a phone call or looked at a text on your mobile while stuck in a traffic jam or waiting at traffic lights?

Any of those 'innocent' little misdemeanours could, if the circumstances went against you, lead to you being detained at Her Majesty's pleasure for a period of time, especially should you be involved in an accident while doing any of the above, and if someone was injured or even killed then you could be looking at some serious time behind bars.

You could be a company director responsible for staff and without your knowledge an unsafe working practice that leads to injury or death becomes common practice amongst the staff, well the law could hold you responsible, even if you had no direct knowledge of the practice and you could be charged and found guilty of manslaughter and end up serving over ten years.

These examples aren't meant to scare you, simply to highlight that many 'ordinary' people, people who consider themselves law-abiding citizens can still end up in prison for many different reasons, and until you've seen the inside of a British prison you have no true idea of the reality that awaits you.

I hope this book pulls back the curtain a little for you.

But let's also be realistic, 70% of custodial sentences are imposed on those with at least 7 previous convictions or cautions, and 50% are imposed on those with at least 15 previous convictions or cautions.

What this means is that 70% of the current 84,000 prisoners in prisons in the UK (which is 59,000) have had at least 7 previous convictions or cautions so were hardly innocent little angels that had never run into trouble with the law before.

Of course, the flip side of that is this means that around 25,000 prisoners had either no (or under 7) negative interactions with the police showing on their criminal record which shows that the courts typically give an individual many chances before they resort to imprisonment in all but the most serious of cases.

Simply put, 7 out of ten prisoners have been in trouble multiple times before, it is relatively unusual for a 'honest' citizen to end up in prison first time out, unless it's related to a fairly serious crime.

Typically the 'average' law-abiding citizen is unlikely to end up in prison but I'm not in the judgement game, I'll admit that earlier in my life I could have ended up on the other side of the law and I think many others could say the same.

I, like many people had the opportunity to make choices in my life and a few of them, had I not been a bit lucky could, potentially, have led to me being on the wrong side of a cell door.

As it turned out, after a few different jobs over the years I ended up working in several of Her Majesty's Prisons, initially as a Prison Officer (never a guard, warder or warden, despite what the media like to call us on occasion), then over the years I climbed up the career ladder before ending up in roles out of uniform but still within the prison system, which has given me a unique perspective on life inside for prisoners (and staff) and how best to navigate the system.

I've tried to order the chapters in this book in the order that, should you be expecting to spend some time at Her Majesty's pleasure, events will most likely unfold for you. If you are already inside then some of the earlier chapters will be of limited use to you but later chapters will still be relevant in one way or another.

If you're about to go inside for the first time this book isn't going to answer every question but it is going to make those first few weeks a lot less confusing and upsetting and hopefully the rest of the stay a lot easier to navigate.

If you're a friend, loved one or simply somebody interested in the system or thinking about working inside a prison then I hope you find the book interesting and informative.

Thanks for reading.

BEFORE COURT

This chapter is about preparing to go to court for sentencing or trial and should be considered if there's *any* chance that you're not going to be going home, but instead may end up in one of Her Majesty's Prisons. To be honest, I would say that it's better to be prepared and anyone who is attending court (or even a police station for bail reasons) would be better off if they were this prepared.

Obviously, if you were arrested at the scene of a crime (or incident), taken from the police station directly to court and then remanded to prison you won't have had time to go out and buy this book, unless you were really thorough in your research of course!

In life it is always better to be prepared and arriving at prison unprepared simply makes the whole process that much more difficult for you (and your loved ones); believe me when I say that your first 2 weeks inside are likely to be the most confusing and stressful time in your life and yet with a little bit of planning ahead you can reduce the stress for both yourself and your family.

- Keys - Make a plan and sort out your keys, the keys to your property, the keys to your car or motorbike, the keys you use in your everyday life. If possible leave spares with someone you trust or where that person can get them easily, getting your keys released to someone from your stored prison property is a slow and complicated process.

- Get a small holdall or backpack that you can put the following items in; it doesn't need to be big or fancy, it's not going to contain much.

- Telephone Numbers List - Write down on at least two pieces of paper (I'd recommend three photocopies) the phone numbers you will want / need whilst in prison. Family, solicitors, friends, landlord, employer, neighbour, whomever you think you might need to call while in prison for any reason, write their name and number down and put each one of these lists in separate places, one in a pocket of something you're wearing to court, one in your wallet and one somewhere else in your personal belongings; this way you should definitely have at least one set of numbers available to you once you arrive at prison. If you've got a good memory then you could try memorising them but nowadays that seems a lost skill, personally I can barely remember my own mobile number, let alone anyone else's.

- Be realistic - If there's *any* chance you're going to be handed a prison sentence then tell your loved ones and others that need to know. Who's going to feed your pets, what about the rent and your furniture and belongings, there's plenty to think about and whilst you may be innocent and hoping the jury will realise that, or guilty and be hoping to get away with something, you need to understand that trying to call your landlord to arrange for your furniture (or at least valuables left in the property) to be secured during your absence will be a lot harder from inside than outside. Understandably you'll probably want to keep as few people informed as possible during this period of your life and in that case you should consider arranging with a trusted family member or friend to deliver letters (or have conversations) with the other people that need to know your situation if a prison sentence is the decision of the court.

- Valuables - Don't wear sentimental or expensive jewellery, don't take a good mobile phone to court or any other high value items. You won't be able to use them in court, you won't have access to them in prison and you're just increasing the likelihood of them being misplaced. If you're out on bail and attending court I'd suggest buying a cheap as possible pay-as-you-go mobile, putting only a couple of numbers on it and only using it on the way to and from court, that way if the judge suddenly decides to remand you or the jury returns a guilty verdict quicker than expected (it can happen) then your £800 mobile doesn't get seized and potentially lost in the system. You need to understand that if you are remanded or sentenced then your jewellery, phone and any other valuables get taken from you at court. From court they then get passed to the prison transport company who will move you to the prison, then the prison staff will receive them and pass them to the valuable property storage department within the prison where they'll be held either until you're released or moved to another prison. That's a lot of people / places for your valuables to get misplaced and I'm afraid that things do get misplaced one way or another sometimes. Even if they're not misplaced, you could wake up in one prison, go to court and at the end of the day end up in another prison and now your valuables have to play catch-up which whilst it should be an automatic process may involve you having to write complaints and 'general applications' to various departments. Alternatively, your case could end without imprisonment and you get released from the court but now you have the aggravation of having to go back to the prison to get your valuables.

In my opinion there's no upside to having your valuables with you, It's not worth it, avoid the hassle, if your only real 'valuable' in the prison is a £10 phone then you can collect it at your leisure, if you can be bothered at all.

- Cash - You are not going to be allowed cash whilst in prison. However, if when you turn up you have cash on you it will be put into your account (more on this later) which means that you'll have the ability to buy certain approved items.

Obviously this all depends on your personal circumstances, how long you're going to be in prison and if you have loved ones or friends who are going to be willing and able to send you money from the outside. For the purpose of this book I'd suggest you carry on you a minimum of £40, this will be enough for you to purchase the 'welcome pack' and some PIN (phone) credit as without these your first week inside will be even harder than it needs to be. If you can afford to bring more money in then do so, although I wouldn't recommend more than £500 unless there's absolutely nobody on the outside who's going to be able to send you money in during the length of your sentence. Don't worry, when you're released you'll be given any outstanding balance.

A word of warning - Don't try to 'hide' the proceeds of crime in your prison account; if you turn up with £20,000 in cash then the Security department and the police will definitely be having a conversation about it.

- Get a haircut - It might sound silly but having a smart appearance at court might help and if it doesn't then not having to pay a fellow prisoner to attempt to cut your hair with clippers for the first month or so will help save you money and give you time to see the wing barbers 'efforts' on others before trusting him with your hair!

- Clothing - Obviously (hopefully) you're going to wear a suit (or be as smart as you can be) for your court appearances but also think about clothing inside. In the small hold-all try to keep a pair of trainers, flip-flops (for the showers), a pair or three of tracksuit bottoms and at least 6 t-shirts / tops (no hoodies, black trousers or white shirts). Unless you really believe going to prison is a fashion show don't waste your money on fancy expensive makes, they're more likely to get stolen (shocking fact, some of your fellow prisoners are thieves) damaged or lost and at the end of the day who are you trying to impress? Don't worry, the prison will supply you with clothing and for the first couple of weeks you might be in just prison clothing anyway. There's always a laundry (quite often on the residential unit) where you can wash / get your own clothes washed or if you're only wearing prison clothes then at 'kit change' (normally once a week) you'll be able to swap dirty for clean clothing and bed linen.

- Photographs - Have at least one decent photograph of your loved ones, no nudity, try to make it a photo that makes you smile and helps you to remember happier times. Make sure the photograph doesn't include you, normally photographs that include your face won't be allowed for security reasons.

- Books - You may not have read a book for years or you may read three per week but trust me when I say you should put a book in your holdall, of course it's up to you what type, it could be a novel, a book to learn a new language, a religious book, it doesn't matter, just have something to read should the desire arise. Most prisons will allow you to bring in a book as long as it's not likely to cause trouble (I'd recommend you don't try to bring in Salman Rushdie's novel The Satanic Verses or Hitler's Mein Kampf as you won't be allowed those or similar books). You will be allowed access to the prison library but this can be fairly erratic and depending on which prison the choice may be limited so don't count on it.

- Smoking / Drugs - If there's any chance you're going to end up in prison then you should try to quit as soon as possible. Getting caught in prison doing either or with the materials will get you disciplined (loss of some privileges) or could end up with you having extra days added to your sentence or even a fresh criminal case (for the more serious drug offences).

Smoking is now banned totally and it's a lot easier to try to quit outside than inside and if you still try to smoke inside you're going to end up smoking either tea leaves in rolled up bible pages, dog ends you found on the floor, tobacco tainted with drugs (particularly Spice) or if you're lucky and find an inside supplier then you'll be buying tobacco at five to ten times the outside cost, this will obviously get you into debt faster than you can say "payday-loans".

Drugs are banned, they're illegal on the outside so obviously they're going to be illegal inside prison. Further, whilst you might know your dealer / supplier on the outside and 'trust' his product, on the inside anything you're offered is going to be ten to twenty times more expensive (yes that's right, ten to twenty times more expensive) for a product of dubious quality, the end result is that you're likely to end up in debt very quickly for a far inferior product with the added likelihood of being disciplined by the prison staff if caught with drugs. Finally, due to the fact that 'Spice' tries to mimic better known drugs but is chemically synthesized people can have bad reactions to it, more on that later.

Now, you might look back on this chapter and feel that it's quite a long list but it's not, it's less than most people have to organise for a 2 week holiday in Spain and unfortunately prison is neither a holiday nor Spain.

So here's the short list, easy for you to make a note of:

Sort out your keys, Small holdall or rucksack, telephone numbers on paper (x3), tell people who need to know, don't bring valuables, bring some cash (minimum £40), get a haircut, some cheap clothes, a photograph, a book and try to quit smoking and / or drugs.

MEDICAL & DENTAL

Healthcare, be it medical or dental is not as easily accessible as it is on the outside. If you thought getting a doctor or dentist appointment was difficult in NHS 'postcode lottery' Britain then prepare yourself for a shock in prison.

Having said that, on most days you'll technically be able to see a nurse if your prison is lucky enough to have a healthcare department (as some of the bigger prisons do) but beyond handing out a couple of paracetamol or booking you an appointment to see a doctor or dentist they're generally there to hand out medication already prescribed and deal with emergency situations until the ambulance arrives.

- Medication - If you're on any medication that you will need to take whilst in prison then make sure you speak to your doctor before so that when the prison contact the surgery to confirm your details and prescriptions there are no problems. Ensure you carry with you to court every day (I'd suggest in original packaging in a clear bag) at least 2 weeks worth of medication and a copy of the prescriptions you currently take, it may not take that long to sort it out but it could. The chances are you won't be allowed to keep the medication with you (in possession) but instead you'll have to attend the 'meds' hatch daily to collect your daily medication from the nurse. Only take prescribed medication, you can't arrive with your own paracetamol, antihistamines or stomach upset medicine unless it's been prescribed by your doctor.

- Dental - Visit your dentist now. Get a complete check-up and anything that looks slightly dodgy, or anything that has given you a bit of trouble in the past and then faded away, get it sorted now. In real life (on the outside) if you wake up with raging toothache you can usually get an emergency appointment within 24 hours and in the meantime buy and try all sorts of painkillers (including alcohol), in prison you could be waiting weeks (or longer) and if you're lucky you may get a couple of normal paracetamol a day to help with the pain, which in my experience with toothache is next to useless! I cannot stress this enough, you do not want to have to wait for dental help in prison, get it dealt with before and then once in prison take care of your remaining teeth obsessively, don't worry, you'll have the time.

COURT OR VIDEOLINK?

Once you have been arrested and the CPS (Crown Prosecution Service) have decided to charge you the matter is then passed to the courts for them to proceed with.

Which court it ends up at will usually depend on the severity of the offence.

There are (summary) offences that are usually deemed suitable for the Magistrates Court to deal with, other offences that are considered triable either way (summary or indictable) which means the magistrates will hear the initial facts of the case and decide if they can deal with it or if they want to pass it up to the Crown Court as their sentencing powers aren't strong enough in the case of a guilty verdict and finally offences (indictable) that the Crown Court deals with as the case is considered to be serious enough that only a Crown Court could try the case and sentence appropriately if a guilty verdict is passed down.

For the vast majority of people who eventually find themselves staying at one of Her Majesty's Prisons they will initially have passed through a Magistrates Court before being passed on to a Crown Court.

Currently the majority of these appearances, and in fact most court appearances are conducted in person, which means that the defendant is physically in the courtroom, standing in the dock in front of the Magistrates or Judge.

I say currently because, over the last 5 years or so, there has been a steady increase in the number of videolink court appearances, conducted between the physical court and a special video enabled video suite in either the prison or even the police custody suite.

This change has increased as technology has become more commonplace and it offers a great saving for the court and prison service in time and money which ultimately means the taxpayer is saving money. The technology used is simply a variation on the software used to make video calls using Skype, Apple Facetime or business video conference software.

The defendant sits in the video booth with a camera (webcam) facing them and a monitor for them to see and hear what is going on in the court and in the court they have monitors that display the accused to the court and multiple cameras that switch between those talking in the court at the relevant times for the defendant to see.

Currently the most common use of this technology is for the court to be able to deal with minor 'procedural' matters and occasionally sentencing as these are often very short hearings that don't make a 2 hour + round trip in a prison transport van (sweatbox) either necessary or beneficial for the defendant. In the case of a jury trial it is still currently more 'normal' for the accused to be there in person rather than to appear by videolink although I suspect that as time progresses videolink trials will become more commonplace as they are a lot more cost and resource effective.

Personally, I feel that anyone who is accused of a crime and appearing in front of a jury by videolink could potentially be put at a disadvantage, which in turn could increase the likelihood of them being convicted.

Imagine that you are sitting on a jury. You are brought into court, sat down in the jury box and you look across to the dock where the accused should be. Let us consider the two possibilities:

Option one - You see a smartly dressed well presented individual who looks to all appearances similar to you and the other jury members. They are there in front of you and during the trial you'll be able to see how they react to every piece of evidence, every bit of body language they exhibit and despite your ultimate decision hopefully being based solely on the evidence provided during the trial, your first impression and ongoing impressions of the defendant may lead you to consider some elements of the case more relevant than other elements.

Option two - You see a large TV monitor with the defendant appearing on it. I would imagine your first thought might be "Why aren't they in court?" followed by possibly frustration that you can't see their entire body language or their complete reactions to evidence or points provided.

I think that many jurors could come to the conclusion that the person isn't attending in person because they're currently in prison, and from there the presumption of innocence has been eroded to a degree. I mean, let's be honest, a typical jury member isn't going to assume the defendant is on holiday and videolinking in for their convenience, the assumption is going to be negative rather than positive.

Now, I'm not saying that videolink appearances are definitively negative but I think that trial by jury via videolink is not an option I would be happy with if I was the defendant.

However, keep in mind that it won't be the prison that decides how you appear, the court will inform the prison if you are to appear in person or via videolink and they will do as the court directs. Your legal team can make representation to the courts for one or the other but the courts have the ultimate decision making power.

R. E. S. P. E. C. T.

Respect is obviously something that most people want, be it from work colleagues, friends, family or people on the street. Lives have been lost for perceived instances of deliberate lack of respect but rarely nowadays is the art of apparent respect more highly practiced than in a Crown Court, and to a lesser degree, inside a Magistrates Court.

If you've never seen it before it can almost look like a play being acted out before you, and to a degree it is, the barristers, the clerks and the judge all know their roles and the language their roles demand.

Barristers usually refer to each other within the court as "my learned friend" or my "my learned colleague".

Everybody in the court, barristers, court clerks and witnesses refer to the judge as "my Lord" or "your Honour".

Language is very carefully considered and controlled, for example a barrister may say:

"I put it to you that your version of events is not quite correct"
or
"I would suggest that you are mistaken"

when speaking to a witness (normally a witness from the opposing side). Basically they're calling the witness a liar, or at least they're saying that they don't believe the version of events the witness is giving. They would never actually call the witness a liar, instead using the above phrases or similar.

Another example is if one barrister says something the other barrister objects to then there's no "Objection" shouted out (as you might expect if you've watched too many legal dramas on TV), the barrister with the objection will simply stand up, the other barrister will notice and stop talking and sit down and the objecting barrister will say something along the lines of "My Lord" (because they'll be addressing the judge), "I find myself at a loss as to why my learned friend is going down this path" or "My Lord, as my learned friend knows, the matter being raised now has already been dealt with" or "My Lord, I feel that my learned friend has started to discuss matters which would best be dealt with in the absence of the jury".

Following this 'outburst' they'll sit down and (usually) the judge will then either make some comment to the first barrister such as "Could we perhaps all agree this matter has been previously dealt with?" or turning to the jury and saying "Please accept my apologies, a matter of law has come up that needs to be discussed. Whilst it is your job to judge the defendant on the evidence presented, it is my job to consider the legal aspects and as such there is no need for you to be involved with this part of the case. The clerk will take you to the waiting area and I would hope we'll have you back in 5-10 minutes. Thank you".

Or the judge may simply raise an eyebrow and look at the other barrister to indicate it's their chance to counter the politely worded objection. In this case the standing barrister will sit, the first barrister will stand, and then they'll say something along the lines of "My Lord, I fear that my learned friend has misunderstood my meaning, I was not implying or suggesting what they seem to believe I meant, I was merely exploring the area of the testimony from the witness in order to clarify the matter for the jury". Now at this stage the judge might say "Very well, as I feel that you've clarified that enough and I'm sure the jury understand what you were trying to get to so let's move on" or maybe "Perhaps your colleague has a point that you do seem to be quite a long way from the point and it would be better to rethink your questions and get back on track".

Either way, the end result is that everyone is ever so terribly polite to each other, and that watching two barristers disagree with each other (one can hardly call it arguing when they're so polite) with the judge being the referee is both entertaining and highly civilised. Even watching a judge tell a barrister off is a lesson in language and tone, with the barrister having no option but to accept the judges words or try to argue in even more flowery terms; I offer this actual exchange I witnessed once when sitting in the viewing gallery (did you know most courts are open to the public to attend?) as an example:

Judge - "I, and I suspect the jury as well, understand what you are trying to get the witness to say, but as you can tell, asking the witness what is essentially the same question 7 different ways doesn't seem to be eliciting the response you hoped for so I would suggest we move on"

Barrister - " My Lord, I have no desire to waste your time, or the jury's or my learned friends but I really feel that this point needs to be clarified as the case rests heavily on this point"

Judge - "And yet, because the witness, despite you asking the question repeatedly in many different ways isn't saying what you hoped for or expected, you appear to believe that continuing to ask may result finally in a response you are happy with. I believe the question has been asked clearly and comprehensively and would strongly suggest that you move on."

Barrister - "Yes, my Lord and I thank the court for its guidance"

Now for that particular exchange I can tell you that even the jury were looking at each other with amusement on their faces, watching the judge squash the barrister and the barrister having to thank him for it!

Anyway, back to the example. You're due to attend court, you've been taken from your cell with all your possessions you had there, taken to Reception where you've checked your other possessions are coming with you, hopefully you've changed for court into something smart (and you will have been subjected to a full search) and then you'll be processed by the reception staff, handed over to the transport company and off you'll go to court in a secure van.

FROM COURT TO PRISON

So (hopefully) you turned up for court smartly dressed, with your holdall or rucksack and the judge or magistrate has (unfortunately) either remanded you in custody or sentenced you to time in prison.

Generally speaking there isn't much difference in how you're going to be treated in prison, (there are a few differences which I will talk about later) and you'll definitely be treated the same by the transport company (usually Serco or GeoAmey currently) who'll be responsible for taking you to prison.

However, I'm jumping ahead a bit, let's go back a stage and look at the reasons for the decision as to whether you've been remanded or bailed (assuming you haven't been sentenced due to a guilty plea or the end of your trial).

It's actually a fairly simple decision for the court and it's normally based on three factors:

- how serious the offence you've been accused of is and the level of likely punishment if convicted, and

- the likelihood of you turning up for your court appearance at a later date

- If you have pled guilty and the likely sentence is a prison sentence

If the accused person has no criminal record, a regular job, stable accommodation and the offense is deemed of a sufficiently low level (no violence, low financial gain, no weapons, no evidence to show specific intent to commit the offence, etc) then typically bail would be granted, sometimes by the police (police bail) and sometimes by the court and being granted this bail would normally involve the person normally having to report to the local police station on a daily or weekly basis to 'sign in'.

If, on the other hand, the accused person has a string of previous convictions or the offense is deemed high level (violence, high financial gain, drugs, weapons, multiple offences or multiple counts of the same offence, etc) then the courts will normally remand the accused in custody, which means the accused is being sent to prison until their trial is completed, unless their legal representative (solicitors or barristers, depending on the court involved) manage to make a bail application to the court which is successful.

If the accused / defendant pleads guilty at any stage, and the likely sentence (including any early plea discount) is likely to result in a prison sentence then the defendant is most likely going to be sent to prison directly from the court. In rare cases an individual may be given some time (days rather than weeks) to get their affairs in order before imprisonment but in over a decade I've only known of that twice and they were both highly 'professional' men who had been sentenced to relatively short (under 12 months) sentences.

For the purpose of this chapter the reason why doesn't matter. If the judge or magistrate has decided that you either need to be remanded into custody or has sentenced you to a custodial (prison) sentence then it's prison you're going to.

A quick word here on prison sentences: Hopefully your solicitor / barrister has explained this but as a 'general' rule you'll serve half of your sentence in prison and the other half out on 'licence' in the community. This doesn't take into account 'HDC - Home Detention Curfew' which is an electronic tagging ankle bracelet that I'll go into more detail in a later chapter.

Our current Prime Minister has pledged to change the half served in-

side, half outside for certain categories of prisoners including people convicted of terrorism related offences and seriously violent offences, if these pronouncements get turned into law we'll have to wait and see as politicians aren't the most reliable at following through on their promises.

Anyway, back to the sentencing aspect, here's an example:

The judge sentences you to 3 years, this means you'll be in prison for 18 months and then on 'licence' for 18 months, during which time you can be recalled back to prison if you fail to meet the licence conditions. If you were remanded (held in prison) for 3 months before and during the trial then that 3 months will be taken off your 'prison' time, so in that case you'd serve another 15 months before being released on 'licence'.

Okay, example finished, let's go back to the court, the judge / magistrate has either just sentenced you or remanded you to prison. Upon hearing this news, don't swear or shout vengeance on the judge, jury or others and don't try to make a run for it, neither will get you very far and definitely won't help you in later days.

You might get a few minutes with your legal team or you might not but you'll be taken to the court cells where you'll be held until the transport is ready. Your holdall / rucksack will be bagged and tagged ready for transport with you. You could be waiting in the court cells for an hour, it could be eight hours, it depends at what time you were taken down and how quickly the transport fills up and is ready to leave.

I'm sure you've seen on the nightly news those white vans carrying a high profile defendant into the Old Bailey with the press trying to take pictures through the blacked out window slots.

Whilst I can't guarantee the paparazzi will be trying to take your picture, I can tell you your transport is going to be very similar and that inside those vans are very small individual transport cells, more like solid plastic cupboards with a bench to sit on, and that you'll be placed in one of those for the journey to your new temporary accommodation, the 'Local' prison.

These vans are known amongst prisoners and staff as 'Sweat boxes' primarily because they're so small and even in the mildest weather they can get quite hot and sweaty. Did I mention they're small? Have you got a small wardrobe in your home, if so then imagine sitting inside it on a hard plastic seat whilst it bumps up and down for an hour or three, with limited ventilation, no entertainment and quite possibly some very noisy neighbours in the van.

It is not fun, it is not meant to be fun, and it makes your local bus, a Ryanair flight or even a 1985 Skoda seem luxurious and you will be grateful to get out of it when you reach your destination, even though that destination is a prison.

ARRIVAL

You have been transported from the court to your 'Local' prison. Now, this might not actually be local to either your home or even the nearest prison to the court you've just come from, but it should be the nearest prison that is set up to accept 'new' arrivals and is thus known as a 'local'.

Unfortunately however sometimes 'local' prisons 'lock out' which means that they inform the courts that they traditionally 'serve' (and the transporting companies) that they are not able to accept any more prisoners (for some reason or another) and in that case people coming from courts may be sent to the next available 'local' prison, which could be 20+ miles away, depending on where you are in the country. This can cause you problems later if you get 'stuck' in a prison not convenient for your family and friends to visit, I'll explain a bit more on that in another chapter.

I'll also explain categories of prisons later but as a 'local' prison is almost certainly going to be the first prison you experience you need to know that they're almost always Category B prisons, which apart from the level of security also means that your fellow inmates might not be the nicest of people (unless your social life really needs a boost, prison is not the place to be making new friends anyway but at the same time it's also not somewhere you should be looking to make new enemies so tread carefully).

Once the transport van arrives at the prison, it will go through a security checking procedure and from there it will go to an unloading area where you'll be removed from the van to a communal holding cell in the Reception area of the prison.

Having worked in Reception in a few prisons I can tell you a few things that might be useful:

- Trying to escape from the unloading area as you get taken from the bus is both pointless and will only end up with you starting your time there in the most negative way.
- Having a bad attitude with (or attacking) the staff. You being in prison is not their fault, being rude or violent with them won't make your life better or easier.
- Prisons are complicated places and if you're stuck in a holding cell waiting to be dealt with then there's a good reason for it, trust me, the staff want to process you and get you sorted out just as quickly as you want it; try to be patient.

Depending on the number of incoming prisoners awaiting processing you could be in this holding cell for a few hours, most local prisons will have incoming from several local courts and often they all turn up around the same time, creating a bit of a bottleneck for the Reception staff and sometimes things occur in other parts of the prison that mean Reception staff can't process you as quickly as they'd like.

This is important and I will repeat it several times throughout this book: Try to be polite to the staff, they're doing a job and getting on their bad side is *never* going to do you any good. I'll go into this in more detail in another chapter.

You will be collected from your holding cell and at the Reception desk staff will check your details with you and the van staff, confirm the possessions bag, separate any valuables you have (hopefully you don't have any apart from the cheap mobile and some cash), itemise the valuables and receipt (make a record of) the cash for addition to your soon to be created prison account. If there's any difference between what they say you have and what you think you should have, now is the time to bring it up politely, trust me when I tell you that getting angry at the staff won't help and nor will complaining about something 5 months later.

You'll then be fingerprinted (electronically) and (now here different prisons operate differently but the most common next step is this) taken back to the communal holding cell where you'll wait until you're collected again.

When collected again it will be for you to be taken to a changing area where you'll change out of the clothes you wore to court, be searched thoroughly with two officers of your gender carrying out the search (you will be naked (technically you won't be naked as the Prison Service has strict rules about full searches but your top half will be naked, and then your bottom half will be naked, but at no time will you be completely naked) so don't think sellotaping 20 Benson and Hedges to your scrotum is a good idea). If you refuse to be searched then more officers will attend and you will be searched whilst under restraint if necessary, no incoming prisoners pass through Reception without having a full search carried out.

Once you have been searched you will get dressed in prison issued clothing. Your court clothing and your holdall possessions will be searched by staff at this point and they will itemise everything, regardless of whether it is given to you as allowed to be in possession or is taken for storage (to be handed back upon release).

Depending on the time of your arrival the next big event will be your introduction to prison food. Assuming like most court arrivals you've arrived late afternoon / early evening this is going to be dinner / tea / supper, call it what you like, it's likely going to be the only hot meal of the day and almost definitely your last meal of the day. Depending on when you last ate, how you're feeling after being sent to prison, and what you're used to eating will greatly influence how you feel about this meal but for most people the fact that it's food, hot (warm) and edible makes it acceptable enough.

Before you get taken to your new accommodation (cell) you'll have a First Night In Prison interview by a prison officer or two (known as the FNIP officers) and also (in a separate room) a quick medical check / chat with a qualified nurse to discuss any medical issues (and make sure you tell them everything medically they might need to know, they don't need to know if you're allergic to cats but if you're on antidepressants or heart medication then they really do need to know!). The FNIP interview covers various things which will help the officers to decide if you need special care and attention due to your state of mind, which accommodation is most suitable for you, and also to answer any specific urgent questions you may have and to offer you the 'Welcome Pack' which contains such basics as tea bags, milk, biscuits etc and may include a 'vape' kit if you are a smoker. This 'Welcome Pack' is not a free gift, the cost will be deducted from your account so keep this in mind although I do recommend you buy a pack to help you through the first week or so. It is normally at this stage that you will be given a temporary PIN code in a sealed envelope that will allow you to make a quick (around 4 minutes I believe) phone call to someone to let them know where you are. If you are given a 'restricted' PIN code then you should be asked at this time to write down the name and number (and relationship) of the person you would like to call, so that the Public Protection Team (more about them in a later chapter) can run their checks prior to you being able to make that call. This is to prevent prisoners calling their victims or witnesses.

Once you've had your FNIP interview and seen the nurse you'll then be temporarily placed in another communal holding room, awaiting officers to take you and others to the Induction Residential wing or houseblock within the prison and this is where you'll be located in a cell. It's here you'll most likely be given a bed pack, a breakfast pack and your cell should already include a mattress, pillow, TV and a kettle.

PHONE CALLS & MAIL

Being able to maintain family ties is viewed as an important element of prisoner rehabilitation, or at least reducing recidivism (which is a fancy word for continuing to commit crime once released and therefore ending up in prison again). With this in mind, prisoners are allowed to make contact with family and friends under controlled conditions. This means that whilst telephone calls, mail and visits are allowed they are carried out under one form or another of surveillance.

Mobile phones of any type are not allowed in prisons. Staff, visitors, prisoners, it doesn't matter, no mobiles are allowed inside and bringing a mobile phone into a prison can result in a large fine and or imprisonment.

The main reason for this is because the prison authorities have several duties of care when it comes to prisoners and their custody and one of those is to reduce the risk of harm to the general public, which is part of the reason for the prisoner being imprisoned after all.

Every prisoner is issued upon arrival a PIN (phone identification number) with enough credit on it to make a quick phone call to tell a loved one which prison they are in. After that phone call, they will have to submit the name, phone number and relationship of anyone they want to be able to call, assuming they have put credit (PIN credit) on their account, to the PIN clerk who will contact the individual(s) listed and ask them if they're happy to receive calls from the relevant prisoner. This entire process can easily take a few days, longer if a weekend gets in the way and it can be very frustrating for new prisoners to have to wait for their numbers to be cleared and made live. The PIN clerk is a civilian member of staff (normally) who works a Monday - Friday work week so getting angry with officers on the residential unit because you're phone numbers aren't 'on' yet is pointless, a polite request for an officer to chase up the PIN clerk is more likely to work if, after a few 'working' days the numbers haven't gone live.

If a prisoner is being held for domestic violence reasons or if the prison is aware of issues in this area then even more care is taken as to who the prisoner is allowed to contact and who is allowed to contact the prisoner and for this reason the verification process can take longer.

All prisoners social calls are recorded with a percentage being listened to, this is only for security reasons and is carried out by the Security Department, not the officers you will deal with on your residential unit. Prisoners calls to proven legal representatives are not listened to.

Prisoners are also allowed to send and receive mail. All incoming mail (with the exception of proven legal correspondence) is opened to ensure no prohibited items are being sent in via the mail. All mail is also subjected to drug detection procedures which may include the use of dogs or current technological methods. Some prisons, including my most recent one, have taken to actually photocopying the original letter and providing the photocopy to the prisoner in order to combat the rise of drug infused paper being used as writing paper.

Prisoners are provided with 2 envelopes and paper and are allowed to send (at the prisons expense 2 second class letters per week. When a prisoner has written a letter they should ensure that they have written the name and address of the person they are writing to on the envelope, and include their own name and Prison number on the back flap and they should not seal the envelope as it may well be checked before staff seal it.

The only exception to this is when a prisoner is sending mail to their legal team / solicitor, in this case they should, once they've completed the letter and envelope, find an officer and ask them to check the contents, they will quickly look (to make sure you haven't written in big red letters "I'm going to kill you" or something similar) or included anything else in the envelope and then they will either seal the envelope themselves or tell you to seal it and they should sign their name across the sealed flap, indicating to the mail room and Security Department that it has already been checked.

Most mail rooms are staffed by OSG's although I understand a few are run with civilian staff but either way, most mail rooms only operate on a Monday to Friday basis, which means if your loved one sent you a letter on Thursday evening, it probably won't get to your residential unit until maybe the Monday or Tuesday afternoon.

NEWSPAPERS & MAGAZINES

Should you have the money and the desire to pay for a daily newspaper or a monthly magazine you can do so or your loved ones on the outside can place an order for you. These deliveries are organised by specially cleared companies for security reasons and due to the process within the prison it is fairly standard for a daily newspaper not to be delivered until the late afternoon or early evening. Personally I'm not convinced of the wisdom of paying for a newspaper that contains news from the day before (as all newspapers do) which you're not going to get until later the following day; when you consider the speed with which TV reports news events nowadays the chances are high that there's barely going to be any 'new' news in the newspaper when it arrives.

Monthly magazines are a different matter as they're usually more specialised, cars, football, hobbies, etc and are less time specific. Also, while adult magazines are generally allowed to be ordered from outside, the rule typically seems to be as long as you could buy it from the top shelf of WH Smith then most prisons will allow it. However, you are not allowed to display any nudity in your cell (although many do and many establishments seem to turn a blind eye to it) and prisoners are not allowed adult dvd's.

Any photographs sent in to a prisoner will be checked by the mail room staff to ensure they don't have a photo of the prisoner, graphic or violent images or nudity of underage persons; this can obviously mean that a 'innocent' photo a mother sends to a father of their child having a bath can be deemed inappropriate and withheld as will any other unsuitable contents.

SEARCHES

Have you ever personally been searched? You may have been watched or touched vaguely at the airport or going into a night-club but those are amateur level searches compared to searches in prison.

At the start of any search you should be asked if you have anything on you that you want to declare. Don't make the mistake of thinking that any of these searches are on a voluntary basis, if you refuse to co-operate more officers will be called and you'll be searched whilst under restraint, never the most comfortable method of doing anything.

As a prisoner you can be subjected to 3 types of search, pretty much at anytime.

The first, and probably the most traumatic for people is a full search. This is a search conducted by at least two officers of the same gender as you, where you will be naked, where your mouth, ears, hair, genitalia and rear are visually inspected to ensure that you have nothing hidden anywhere. Now, when I say naked, as I explained earlier you'll never actually be fully naked, you'll remove your top clothing, handing it to one officer who will check the clothing for hidden articles whilst the other officer asks you to open your mouth and move your tongue so he can see inside it, then to turn your head to the left, and then the right so he can see in your ears, then he'll ask you to run your fingers through your hair (backwards and forwards) to ensure nothing is hidden and to lift your arms to make sure that you're not hiding anything in your armpits. The other officer will then hand back your top and once you've put that on you'll then be told to remove your footwear, trousers and underwear. Once again these items are passed to one officer who'll check them carefully whilst the other officer will visually inspect you and ask you to do some things that to be honest you won't feel comfortable doing. This will usually include, lifting your penis away from your scrotum, peeling back your foreskin (yes, I've seen sim cards hidden there), lifting your scrotum and pulling apart your rear cheeks (because some people like to put mobile phones or drugs up their anus) and possibly squatting and coughing (anything just inside your anus will probably pop out at this stage) before being handed back your clothes and footwear, The reason it's all done like this is to ensure (or try to reduce) the number of prohibited items coming into prison and by doing you in two halves it's supposed to be less humiliating than standing there completely naked. I've never been searched in this manner myself (but I've had to conduct hundreds of these searches) so I can't say how demeaning it is for the prisoner but trust me when I say the officers aren't enjoying it and we'd rather that it wasn't a necessary part of our job.

The second type is a rub-down search, this is much more like what you may have experienced in a nightclub or at an airport, although it's generally a little more thorough. The officer conducting the search (and there should be two, one rubbing you down and the other checking your footwear and any items you had in your pockets) will usually ask you to rub your hands through your hair, and then using a combination of an electronic scanner (wand) and their hands proceed to search you to ensure no illicit items are present.

The third type of search is the cell search. Your cell is your home, possibly a single cell, probably a double cell, but either way it's the only 'private' area you have whilst in prison and prison officers can, and will, regularly come into your cell and search through all of your possessions looking for illicit articles.

On an almost daily basis they should carry out an "Accommodation Fabric Check" which is more commonly known as "Beds, bolts and bars" where they should check that the bars (or similar) on the windows are secure (so no attempts to file through those bars please), make sure you haven't made any holes in the walls (no Shawshank Redemption style escapes) and also check that the general living space is habitable by ensuring the toilet, sink, taps, lights and Emergency Alarm Bell are working. Now, if when they walk in or during their look around they happen to see anything prohibited then you're going to lose it, possibly be put on a charge and more than likely it will lead to a full search of both you and your cell which will involve practically every item within the confines of your cell being inspected to ensure that it's not hiding more illicit items (mobile phone, charger, drugs, etc). Should something be found then it will depend on whether you're in the cell on your own or sharing and exactly where the item(s) was found, so if you're in a double cell and the item is found hidden in the tv or behind the toilet then you'll both be charged probably unless one of you admits that it's your item. This is why you should do all you can to make sure there's nothing in your cell that shouldn't be, and should resist any attempts by other prisoners to get you to 'hold' something for them.

I've seen hollowed out shelving, tinned food cans crafted to look full, mattresses or pillows partially hollowed out, hollow trainer heels, you name it, I've seen it and the officers will always find it in the end.

When the hiding place has been found, not only do prisoners lose their precious (and usually seriously overpriced) contraband, they'll also be charged and be brought before one of the governors to have the charge adjudicated. If found guilty then they'll be punished in some manner, see the chapter on adjudications for more information on this aspect.

YOUR CELL (AND CELLMATE)

Upon your arrival on the wing / houseblock where Induction (Induction is where over the first few days you'll be introduced to the workings and rules of the prison) takes place prisoners are held in an available room or area until they are allocated a specific cell.

I'm not going to talk about cell sizes because different prisons have different sizes depending on when they were built but they usually always come in two versions, the single or the double, with the vast majority being a double, but there are quite a few prisons where a double may be a single with bunk beds rather than a larger room with two single beds.

First of all you need to know these cells are small. Think of the smallest bedroom in an average flat or house, throw in a bunk bed (if it's a small double), a small wardrobe, a table, a chair and a small TV and if you're lucky add a toilet and sink (not all prisons have in-cell toilet facilities believe it or not) and that's your typical cell.

A 'large' double in prison is maybe the size of a good sized single bedroom on the outside, with two single beds and the other stuff mentioned above.

You're probably going to be spending between 15 and 23 hours every day locked in there, with a small window (barred) for ventilation and not a lot else to do so it's a good idea if you get on with your cell mate from the start if possible.

It's normally only in special specific circumstances that prisoners are allocated a single cell and whilst some see it as a blessing many see it as a curse as people are generally social animals and even though you're not in prison to make friends it apparently becomes very hard time if you don't even have someone to chat to. Regardless, it's not going to be your choice as to the accommodation you're allocated, you're not booking a hotel room after all, although if you get on OK with one of the other people from court (or the holding rooms) then you can always ask the Reception or FNIP officers at that stage or the first officers you see on the Induction unit if you can share and dependant on the availability they may allow it.

Once you've been allocated a cell you'll normally be given a bed pack which will contain a sheet, pillow case, blanket, possibly some more prison clothing (kit), soap, toothbrush and toothpaste, toilet paper, safety razor and deodorant and of course, hopefully a breakfast pack.

The breakfast pack will most likely not fill your heart with happiness, nor your stomach with food I'm sorry to say. It will have a small bag containing some cereal (coco pops, cornflakes, etc), some milk in a carton, some tea bags and sugar. This is not a big breakfast and it's why I recommended you buy the Welcome Pack during the FNIP process in Reception, as at least you'll have something else to eat that evening or the first morning.

When you arrive at your cell you'll enter it and be locked in for the night. The officers that take you to your cell should show you the ECB (Emergency Cell Bell) and inform you of its purpose. In case they don't I'll run through the basics now; it's for emergencies only, if you or your cell mate need urgent medical assistance then press it. If you want to know what time it is, what time you're getting out in the morning or complain that the TV isn't working, then these are not emergencies and officers tend to get a little irritated answering non emergency cell bells. Prison is not a hotel and the officers are not your room service waiters and they are quite within their rights to allocate you a red mark on your file for improper use.

Think of it this way; at night there'll typically be one or maybe two staff patrolling an area with maybe 200 prisoners locked in their cells. If you fall off your bunk and bash your head, or start having a heart attack and need urgent assistance, how happy do you think you'll be if they're answering other ECB's because prisoners have pushed them for trivial matters? Or if you become known as someone who's always pushing their ECB for non-emergencies then that 'could' slow down the officers response rate the one time that you really need it.

Hopefully you'll have a working toilet and sink, a mattress and pillow on your bunk, a working TV and a light that switches on and off. If your cell already has someone else living there and you can't see a mattress or pillow it's likely they've 'borrowed' it. Just ask politely for it, everyone's had a first night in prison and most prisoners will be fine about it. Note that I suggest politeness, in my experience people react better to politeness than 'attitude'; start off with a bad attitude and your cellmate may react in the same way, and he may be bigger or meaner than you!

Now, depending on the time that you turn up at the cell, if you do have a cell mate the chances are they're going to want to chat, they're going to want to 'share' whatever you've got and they might offer to 'share' something with you.

My advice, don't borrow or buy anything to begin with, by all means share some of your stuff if you feel friendly but don't accept anything from anyone else until you know them a bit better. Since the smoking ban started things have changed but the 'standard' rate of interest for borrowing tobacco / rollups was typically 100% per week, meaning that if you borrowed 10 rollups you repaid with 20 within the week, and if you failed to pay then you might get a little physical reminder and your debt would double again to 40. Pretty easy to get in debt and very difficult to get out of it, so my advice is don't borrow in prison....ever.

When it comes to chatting, be careful what you say, you may or may not be a criminal and they may or may not be a criminal but it's best once again to keep it all very vague and general until you know them a bit better. Just explain it's been a very tiring stressful day and most will understand, every prisoner has had a first night in prison.

Oh, a word of warning, it's going to be noisy, probably the noisest place you've ever tried to sleep in. Your neighbours are going to be shouting across the landing to friends, someone's possibly going to be either screaming or kicking their door half the night and your cell mate may want to watch TV until one in the morning. My advice, roll up two bits of toilet paper, stick them in your ears and try to get some sleep, it's going to be a confusing, irritating, boring day tomorrow.

INDUCTION

The Induction process varies for prison to prison but all of them cover the same ground essentially. You will have to attend talks and presentations about the prison rules and what you can expect from the prison and what the prison expects from you. Most prisons have prisoners employed as Induction Peers and they will generally run the Induction with an officer in attendance.

It will also be explained to you about what jobs or education opportunities exist within the prison and how you can apply.

Some prisons induction processes will tell you about how to change your prison kit (usually once a week), how to get clothes brought in, how to book visits (or how your friends and relatives can), how to get money sent in, how and when to order canteen, gym timetables, library access and a host of other things relevant to the particular prison.

Be warned, the quality of Induction does seem to vary greatly across the prison estate from what I've seen so if after the Induction process you still have unanswered questions then do ask the staff.

If you are on an induction group where you are the only "new" prisoner and the rest of the group have already served previous prison sentences then the peers giving the presentation may gloss over most of it as the "audience" won't be paying attention anyway. If you don't understand or want to know something ask the Induction peers or the officer.

As part of your induction process, although not normally as part of a group, you will meet with someone from the chaplaincy team to ask about your religious requirements, the drug team to find out if you have a substance issue, the medical team, mental health team, education, probation and possibly the gym team.

The chaplaincy team deal with your religious and spiritual well-being. There will be people to help every major faith and can often be a source of support for prisoners. They will be able to tell you the times of the religious services held at the prison, and can arrange with your wing officers for you to be able to attend these and they should be able to provide you with a copy of your religions books or texts. Even if you are not actively religious on the outside many prisoners find that inside it provides a level of support they are grateful for so don't dismiss it without considering it.

The drug team within the prison are important. Even if you have no history of substance abuse, and your crime was not drug (or alcohol) related you must meet with the team. If you fail to do so, it can be a "negative mark" against your prison records which could count against you when your time for release on HDC or probation is due for consideration. If you do have drug or alcohol issues, they are able to help you, if you are willing to engage with them.

The medical team will give you a very quick medical check. Don't expert private healthcare levels of attention, they are just concerned with your basic wellbeing and in deciding if you are medically capable of attending work or education.

Education within prison forms a large part of the daily regime. The education department will normally ask you to complete a questionnaire about your educational background and then ask you to take a series of tests to show your English and Maths levels.

All prisons (except Cat D) offer classes to improve your reading and maths levels, including English as a Foreign Language. They also typically offer a wide variety of different courses depending on which prison you are held, but such courses can include Plumbing, Bricklaying, Customer Service, Decorating, Information Technology (computers) and Barbering.

The education department within the prison is focussed on helping prisoners to gain qualifications as it is hoped that with increased education and more qualifications prisoners are more likely to be able to find jobs in the future and therefore be less likely to reoffend.

Probation is an integral part of the prison system. Most prisoners serve only a proportion (normally 50%) of their sentence in prison, with the remainder being 'served' on probation whilst living and working outside. During your first few weeks in prison you should meet with someone from the probation office who will inform you what courses and aims you need to achieve whilst in prison to aid your safe and law abiding return to society. Remember that when released from prison you will most likley be subject to the monitoring and control of the probation service and if you fail to follow their rules then they can recall you to prison, either for two to 4 weeks in the first instance for relatively minor issues or to serve the remainder of your sentence in the case of serious breaches or new offences.

The gym within a prison is usually a well used facility. Like most gyms on the outside, you have to attend a gym induction where you will be shown how to use the equipment before you are eligible to go to the gym. In most prisons there is a restriction on how many prisoners can attend the gym and there are usually waiting lists. Also, keep in mind that although you may want to go to the gym daily the practicalities of prison life mean one or two visits a week is usually the maximum. Even if you are not interested in keeping fit do complete the gym induction as you may change your mind in the future.

THE OTHER PRISONERS

If you've never been in prison before then you're going to be quite shocked by the different types of people in prison.

First of all there's you, and as you know you so I won't go into detail about you but there are many others apart from you and a lot of them won't be similar to you.

I'm not talking about race, of course there are people of practically every colour represented, there are also different ethnicities as well, a white prisoner might be of English, Welsh, Polish, Romanian. American or of Gypsy / Traveller heritage, a black prisoner may be from Africa, the Caribbean or may be born and bred in Britain but of African or Caribbean descent, then there are gang members (more prevalent in London prisons) for whom gang allegiance is stronger than race identity; in fact there can be so many sub-groups that it's difficult to navigate and it's not for the most part relevant if you keep your attitude toned down. You may not get on well with people from one group or another or there may be somebody who decides they don't like you because of the colour of your skin or religious beliefs, my advice is don't be confrontational, things can escalate very quickly in prison and there's no advantage to making enemies in such an enclosed environment.

Possibly the biggest shock for you will be the amount of prisoners who have obviously had very limited education or have issues that a psychiatrist would be better off dealing with.

Lack of education of course doesn't mean anything in particular, I've met some very nice people with barely any education and some very bad people with university educations but let's not forget where you are; you're in prison and generally most people don't end up in prison because they're well adjusted productive intelligent members of society. Just keep in mind that people who have a low IQ or very poor education won't necessarily act in what you would consider a 'normal' way, they may do things that you consider stupid, short-sighted or self-destructive. It's not your place to set them right or interfere, typically they won't thank you for it and more than likely will take offence, it's safer to keep your distance or interact as little as possible with them.

Now, you may be asked to read or write something for someone if you can read and write reasonably well (and if you don't think that you can but are able to read this book then trust me when I tell you that your reading skills are definitely better than around 70% of the other prisoners) and I would always recommend that you do this to be 'nice' rather than for a 'price' as whilst you're not in prison to make friends, having a reputation as someone that helps other prisoners gets you more allies (and protection) than ripping people off for their meagre possessions. A word of warning though, as you're reading it, keep in mind what you're reading and the environment, if it's a letter from a partner breaking up with the prisoner for example then don't read it out loud or gossip about it with others.

Prisoners that need (or appear to need) psychiatric help are a different matter entirely and I'd strongly suggest extreme caution around them, I've seen prisoners go from calm to homicidal in seconds, from extreme murderous rage to calm (scary) laughter in the blink of an eye and it rarely ends with a happy ending. Whilst there is almost always a mental health team within a prison who attempt to help those individuals the fact of the matter is that they're understaffed and unable to deal comprehensively with people with a mental illness. There's also the issue of 'temporary' mental illness which is usually drug induced but I'll go into that in more detail in a later chapter.

Just remember this, regardless of the reason you're in prison (or about to end up in prison) and your innocence or guilt, the vast majority of prisoners are in prison for not being nice, trustworthy, friendly, well-adjusted people.

There may be a burglar who appears to be nice and friendly, you can't trust him, it's possible he'll be a pad thief (someone who steals from other prisoners), there could be a drug addict who'll be friendly to you until you refuse to 'lend' / give them something they ask for in order to fund their next fix, they'll lie to you, steal from you because of their need.

Then there will be the domestic violence / partner abuse inmates. This was one of the more depressing aspects of my job, when looking through prisoner files I would estimate that 1 in 3 prisoners would have some previous or current criminal matter related to domestic violence, regardless of whatever else they might be in prison for. It is not unusual for a drug dealer, burglar or robber to also have a restraining order listed against them from a partner, past or present.

This was shocking to me, but what made it more so was the number of women who were named in these restraining orders but would try to contact or visit the prisoner, against the court order made to protect them!

Of course, the prisoners with such issues would always claim they hadn't meant to hit their partner it had been an accident, they weren't harassing their ex-partner, it was all a misunderstanding, or that she'd wound him up and he'd hit her once in a fit of temper (or whilst drunk) and regrets it every day; now as a prisoner you're not going to get to see their record but I guarantee having seen thousands of these 'misunderstood' mens files over the years I can tell you two things for certain:

1. Unless it was a very serious single event, the vast majority of these men will have been warned by the police

and or courts multiple times before having a restraining order made against them or receiving a custodial sentence.

2. They typically will have previous offences for previous partners or when released will not have learnt their lesson and will come back to prison.

VIOLENCE & SEX

On your first day (or first few days) I would suggest that you should keep your head down.

This isn't a movie where if you pick a fight with the biggest prisoner and win you'll have the respect / fear of the whole prison; the reality is you'll probably end up in healthcare or the local hospital having been taught a lesson by one or more of the prisoners, there's no such thing as a 'fair fight' in prison, no fighting here by The Queensbury Rules or any other idea of chivalry, you're more likely to get hit around the head with a can of tuna in a sock than be involved in a fair fight.
Even if you should win then you'll probably end up in the Care and Separation Unit (otherwise known as the Seg (Segregation) or the Block) for starting / being involved in a fight, you'll lose your TV privileges and if / when you get returned to normal housing you'll be forever watching your back for the next idiot who decides to take you on, or the original guy will want his revenge (normally with friends lending support).

Instead, keep your head down, be reserved (answer questions simply and without attitude), don't borrow (or accept) anything from other prisoners as you don't want to get in debt and just try to keep an eye out to work out who are the troublemakers, the idiots and the mentally unstable. It's sad to say but if you can't spot people from one of those groups it's possibly because you're in one of those groups.

Fortunately in British prisons forced sexual activity is incredibly rare, I can count on one hand the number of claimed rapes that

I've heard of in establishments I've worked in although I'm not saying there isn't unreported incidents or some consensual activity going on that officers don't hear about.

There is one type of assault that does happen which whilst not sexual in nature does get classed as indecent assault (when reported) and although it is not common it is a lot more common amongst certain types of prisoners than others.

I would suggest that if you happen to be eating while reading this you might want to stop (either eating or reading) for the moment as this might make you feel sick.

Ready...?

Okay, here we go...

The incident is called 'spooning' and it generally occurs to prisoners who have come into the prison in the last 48 hours, they are typically drug users or people who live on the street outside (homeless) and they have normally served more than one prison sentence before.

These prisoners will be restrained by between 2 and 6 prisoners, their underwear will be pulled down and a spoon (or something similar) will be inserted into their anus to 'scoop' out packages of drugs or very small mobile phones that they placed there before coming into prison.

Let me expand on that situation a little bit. Someone who is homeless or has a substance abuse issue will be approached by someone who wants to get something prohibited into prison. Alternatively it may be a more 'standard' individual who is out on bail but imminently due to be sentenced to imprisonment that is approached.

Just like drug mules swallowing condoms with cocaine these people do it for the money, although it's a little more complicated than just swallowing and sometimes threats play a part rather than or as well as money.

Firstly they need to 'pack' as much stuff inside themselves as possible, whilst being able to walk without items dropping out. They also need to ensure that their regular toilet habits are interrupted so a few Immodium or similar are taken to ensure the goods don't get flushed down the toilet by accident. Then it's off to either commit a crime or to do something to activate a recall, the end result being them being sent to prison as quickly as possible for hopefully as short a time as possible, in the region of 14 to 30 days is normally the acceptable range.

Once in prison they go through the Reception security procedure, which as good as it is (and it's getting better every week as new technology comes through) can't always detect internal packages (although mobile phones are pretty easy for the detectors) and then they're on a residential unit.

The prisoners inside who are working with dealers on the outside know who is coming and what they should have 'hidden' and aren't necessarily known for their patience or their trusting natures and therefore the spoon method will be used.

Occasionally, because there are rival dealers (and gangs) both inside and outside prisons, an unlucky prisoner who 'fits' the usual couriers profile may be jumped and 'spooned' by a group trying to hijack their competitors delivery but this prisoner may well have nothing to give up, apart from their dignity and while there are those that try to fight off their attackers and those that quietly submit; I can not judge either as having never been in that position, and having seen the extra injuries those that fought sometimes received, and the shame that some who didn't fight exhibit afterwards I do not know which strategy is best.

Having said all that, for the average prisoners who are not involved in gangs or drugs and generally keep their heads down the chance of being subjected to violence are relatively low, in fact, as an officer I would say that I saw more injuries due to prisoners harming themselves than through being attacked by others.

SELF HARM & SUICIDE

Let me be clear, intentional suicide is not common in prison. A prisoner has more people looking at, and after them, in a prison than many people do on the outside and officers (and other staff) receive specialised training to identify and monitor those who either state or exhibit suicidal tendencies. Unintentional suicide is possibly more common but once again, marginally so.

Sadly the mainstream media and charities tend to focus on suicides in prison and compare percentages of suicides in prison populations against public general populations in order to claim that care, safety, training and the environment inside prisons leads to increased suicides.

I'm not a university funded scholar looking at all the socio-economic aspects but as an ex-officer I can tell you several things for sure when comparing 1000 prisoners inside a prison with 1000 people from the general population outside a prison (even if you only look at males aged between 21-30, for example).

Prisoners on average, when compared to people not in prison, have:

- More mental health issues
- More substance abuse issues (drugs or alcohol)
- Less education or qualifications
- Less options on a daily basis, ranging from when to wake up, what and when to eat, communicating with others, access to outside open spaces, media diversions
- Been separated from loved ones and friends
- A greater chance of being a victim or perpetrator of

violence
- Been placed in an environment that is comparable to the worst neighbourhoods on the outside
- Had their future opportunities restricted by the criminal record
- No immediate positive outlook

What this list shows, I believe, is that prisoners are not typical members of the general population and I am sure that if studies were carried out comparing prisoners with people more similar to them then the figures might show that actually suicide in prison is actually suprisingly low, and quite possibly lower than that affecting the outside population.

However, let's look at self harm also. Now I would say that many of the reasons listed earlier are also relevant to prisoners who self harm with one significant difference. A large percentage of prisoners who self harm do it either for the attention or as an attempt at coercion, along the lines of "If you don't give me a cigarette I'm going to cut myself" or something similar, whereas in the general population I believe that most self-harm is carried out by teenage girls or young women and whilst self-harm is more common in the female estate it is still suprisingly high in the male estate compared to the outside male population. Whether this is because it is more easily identified in prisons or reported I can not say.

Self-harm is normally defined as the intentional, direct injuring of body tissue, done without the intent to commit suicide.

Other terms such as "cutting" and "self-mutilation" are also used for any self-harming behavior regardless of suicidal intent. The most common form of self-harm is using a sharp object (which in prison may actually be a fairly blunt plastic knife) to cut the skin. Other forms can include behaviour such as burning, scratching, or hitting body parts and can also include behaviour such as interfering with wound healing, excessive skin picking, hair pulling and the swallowing of certain substances or objects (such as batteries or razor blade fragments from safety razors).

Behaviour associated with substance abuse and eating disorders are not normally considered as self-harm because the resulting tissue damage is typically an unintentional side effect.

Although suicide is not the intention of self-harm, the relationship between self-harm and suicide is complicated as self-harming behaviour can be potentially life-threatening.

Depending on the type of self harm there is an increased risk of suicide in individuals who self-harm and a history of self-harm is found in approxiamately 50% of suicides in the general population. However, stating that individuals who self-harm are likely to be suicidal is, in the majority of cases, inaccurate although the risk of accidental suicide is also increased.

British prisons and their staff take self harm and suicide risks extremely seriously. One of the main obligations on a prison and its staff is to keep prisoners safe and there are multiple methods they employ to do this.

Let's try to look at this in some sort of order:

- When you first come into prison your mood and answers are assessed by the Reception staff, during the First Night in Prison interview process, the medical interview / examination and the staff on the Induction Residential Unit. If any of them suspect, either by your words or actions that you may attempt suicide or self harm then they will open an ACCT (Assessment, Care in Custody and Teamwork) document which is a folder that details various things but also ensures that you are checked on more regularly than you would be otherwise, to ensure you come to no harm. This document also record all interactions with staff and any observed behaviour that may indicate the state of mind. This will be reviewed regularly by specially trained staff who liaise with medical and mental health personnel.

●   Prisoners who have just been sentenced to a long term of imprisonment, prisoners on the anniversary of the death of a loved one (or being sentenced) or any other traumatic / negative events happening in their life such as parole being refused, additional charges being laid, etc which can all be triggers for self harm and as such staff will take care to pay special attention at these times when aware of them.

REMAND OR CONVICTED

You end up in prison for one of two reasons.

1. You've been arrested under suspicion of committing a criminal offence and the legal system (police, Crown Prosecution Service, Court) feels that either for public safety or because they don't believe that you'll turn up to court that you need to be remanded to prison, where you'll wait until your court case (which can easily be many months away) takes place.
2. You've been convicted of a criminal offence and the court has imposed (or has indicated it will shortly impose) a custodial sentence on you which means that you're going to prison (generally for half the declared sentence which we'll look at in a later chapter).

Now, there used to be more of a difference as to how you were treated in prison if you were on remand, rather than convicted, mostly based on the idea of "innocent until proven guilty", but in my experience over the last 10 years or so there's definitely less difference than there used to be in the treatment between the two groups.

The few differences that remain include remand prisoners having more social visits than convicted prisoners and having the ability to spend more on their 'canteen' if the money is available.

There's one important factor that many prisoners don't understand initially that can be quite relevant. If you plead guilty at any stage (usually at the suggestion of your legal team in order to receive a lighter / reduced sentence) and the judge delays your sentencing but feels that going to prison is a strong possibility then you will be held on what is referred to as Judges Remand. This is not the same as remand where you are still claiming innocence, and the prison will treat someone on Judges Remand in the same way as a sentenced prisoner.

TIME

You may have heard the expression *Time is relative* and a fairly normal example of this is that time seems to fly when you're having fun (or busy) but seems to drag when you're not.

Prison time is not fun (busy) time.....at all.

Many people may think that serving time is different from any other experience but the sad fact is that prison time is boring; mind numbingly boring.

However, to try to cheer you up a little bit can I suggest that when you think about it, the truth is that a lot of the time we spend in our lives is boring time.

Take work, whether it's working in a shop, sitting at a desk in an office or any other form of standard employment that people tend to do, all it really comes down to exchanging your time for some money.

Lawyers and business owners may get a lot more money than shop assistants but the truth is that we live our lives exchanging our most precious resource, time, for money to quite often buy things we don't really need in our lives. But that's a different subject.

Anybody who's ever held a job for more than a month or two will agree that most jobs become repetitive, dull, and boring. Even in roles such as police officers, or doctors, or firemen where there's a lot of variety there will also be a lot of boring repetitive elements to their jobs.

In prison, as a prisoner, I'm sorry to say that you will be bored beyond belief. Even if you manage to get one of the more active prisoner jobs, such as a peer, or working in the gardens, you'll still on average only be out of your cell for a maximum of 10 hours per day, probably significantly less. The other 14+ hours a day you'll be locked in your cell, probably with a cellmate and a small TV and not much else.

Think about this for a minute, when you are on the outside, you talk to your partner, your friends, your colleagues, and you typically talk to them about things that happened to you, or that you saw, when you weren't with the person / people you are currently talking to. You'd also check your mobile phone, update your Facebook or whatever, watch a YouTube video, WhatsApp your friends, go down the pub, you're free to do what you want.

If you'd spent all day with your partner, you're unlikely to talk about how you spent the day with them later that day, they were there after all,k so they don't want or need to hear it. Unless you and your cell mate agree to watch the same TV programme and then discuss it later, or you or they had a particularly thrilling day planting carrots in the prison garden then there really isn't that much to talk about with someone who is (and should remain to a point) mainly a stranger. Don't forget, in the vast majority of cases you're not going to know the person in your cell beyond what they (or other prisoners) have told you. You won't know what they're in prison for, what they've been convicted of before, what they've done but never been convicted for, and what they're capable of doing in the future.

This isn't meant to make you paranoid but (to use an American expression) don't overshare with someone in prison, you never know how it could come back to haunt you.

INCOME, EMPLOYMENT & EDUCATION

In prison, having time out of your cell and having money to spend on canteen are two of the biggest day to day concerns most prisoners have, with time out of cell being generally the biggest priority.

The only options available to you for prolonged periods of time out of your cell are education or employment, it is rare for prisoners to do both but not completely unheard of, depending on the employment and education available in the prison.

A word of warning here about working in prison, you are not going to be paid well, depending on what you do and how many hours you do it you will be paid between around £5 - £20 per week, yes, that's right, per week! However, if you have no savings and no other form of income, then to be honest something is better than nothing, and for a lot of prisoners the time out of their cell is more important than the pay received for the job they do.

If you choose to work then be aware the work which you will be allocated in prison will depend on various factors and varies from prison to prison. In all prisons there are the standard jobs of wing cleaner, tea boy (a prisoner that keeps prison officers supplied with tea and hopefully cooks an amazing weekend breakfast) library orderly, kitchen worker etc along with work which can range from making window frames, oeratingas call centre workers (without access to callers details) or packing plumbing parts. When you apply for employment you can express your preference but don't be shocked if you don't get your first choice!

Again it varies from prison to prison but you will be expected to remain at the job you were given for a minimum of 4 weeks before asking for a transfer to another job. Some jobs require more security clearance than others so it can be frustrating at times.

If you choose to go down the education route then you will actually be paid (although not much) for gaining an education (in modern Britain that doesn't happen too often!) after being assessed to determine if the course or class you're requesting is suitable for you and if it is then you'll be put on the list for the next available slot; depending on the course this could mean you're going to be waiting for anything from a couple of weeks to a few months, all I can say is have patience and remember, it's not the officers on your residential units fault that the education or employment department haven't offered you a position yet.

FOOD

Now, I don't know what your idea of a good meal is. It may be that you love McDonalds or KFC, you may dream of a spicy Indian or a great Chinese, it might be a lovely roast dinner courtesy of your mum or it could be a fancy restaurant with a different wine served with each course.

We all have our favourite types of food but prison food is none of these things.

I have never met, in all my years whilst working in prisons, a single inmate who loved the food provided inside, actually, I don't know why I said 'love', I've never met anyone who even liked it and that includes people who think a donner kebab or pot noodle is 'fancy' cuisine.

Nobody goes to prison for the food, although I have seen some people who have benefitted from the food by losing a good few stone (20+ kilos) over a 6 month period, definitely closer to their ideal BMI (body mass index / ideal weight) when they leave than when they arrived but that's a 'positive' side effect of the food (and portion size) and not really a recommendation or comment on the taste.

Whilst you may have come across a 'fine dining' element during comprehensive research of British prisons or prison life, it will, without doubt, be in reference to something called "The Clink". I can assure you that as a prisoner you won't be getting that food, it's a charity run 'rehabilitation' project operating in only a few prisons around the country where a very small number of prisoners get to learn how to cook and present 'decent' level restaurant food.

As a prisoner you will get 3 meals a day although you may not recognise two of them as meals....and here's a word of warning, for the first 5-10 days inside you're likely to be on the 'default' menu, which means that your choice of food won't be your own during that period.

Let's start with breakfast, which typically consists of a small milk carton containing about ½ pint, a small plastic bag containing about 30g (just over an oz) of cereal (it could be porridge, cornflakes, coco pops or rice krispies), a few teabags and sugar / sweeteners.....and that's it. The days of cooked breakfasts are long gone and if you have no idea how small a 30g cereal portion is then just go to the supermarket and look at those tiny boxes you can buy for children, they're usually around 30g each (although they're usually sold in multi-packs).

There's no toast, seconds or fry-ups, just a childs size portion of cereal. Oh, and you'll typically collect your breakfast pack when you collect your evening meal at around 5pm the day before.

Lunch, depending on the prison, will either be delivered or collected between 11am-1pm and will be typically either be a 9" (23cm) baguette with your choice of filling (chosen a week earlier) of processed chicken roll, fish (mackerel), cheese, egg or some other random filling), or a packet of dry flavoured noodles (just add hot water if your kettle is working) which are like Pot Noodles gone cheap and nasty. With either choice you'll also receive a packet of crisps, a fruit flavoured drink carton and a piece of fruit (usually an apple or banana).

The evening meal, usually collected anytime between 4.30pm-7pm depending on the establishment will also be something you 'choose' around a week earlier. There is usually a choice of a meat dish (chicken drumstick or quarter, hamburger, lasagne, meat bolognese, or something similar, a fish dish (maybe steamed fish or breaded fish or a tuna casserole) or a vegetarian option (vegetable bake etc). There will also be potatoes or rice, vegetables, a slice of bread (or two) and either a piece of fruit or some sort of pudding.

The quality of the food (and quantity) will probably remind you of school lunches or some other mass produced canteen style, being bland in flavour as well as being a small portion that all but guarantees that come 8pm around half the prisoners will have also eaten their breakfast pack as a 'snack', meaning that come breakfast they have nothing to eat and must wait for the baguette / noodle lunch to arrive.

If you think that the menu and portions don't sound very inspiring or satisfying then you'd be right, but you need to understand that the food budget per prisoner per day is currently about £2. Yes, that's right, a whole £2 per day per prisoner. £2 will just about get you a cheese baguette in your local supermarket so the prison kitchens actually do quite well to produce something approaching 3 meals a day!

If you stop to think about it, £2 per day to feed an adult equals £14 per week.

How many people outside of prison are visiting food banks claiming their benefits / Universal Credit are so low that their children would starve without foodbanks? Even Child Benefit pays over £20 per week for the first child and around £14 for other children which means that parents 'should' be able to feed their children just using the Child Benefit money, regardless of any other incoming benefits.

I myself have had to budget on occasions and by buying pasta, rice, potatoes, other vegetables, meat on offer, tinned fish and eggs have managed to eat for around £20 per week and I neither starved or went hungry. Anyway, back to the point, food in prison is not particularly tasty or plentiful (although there's normally spare rice / potatoes available if you're at the back of the queue) and I've never seen any prisoners become obese in prison, but it will keep you alive, if not satisfied.

If you're on a special diet, for medical or religious reasons then this will be catered for, although it may take the kitchens a week (or more) to get the message and regularly provide the right food for you.

As you can imagine, prison is not a food destination and to add more quantity and flavours to your food intake you will need to buy extra from 'the canteen' which is the prison version of a supermarket delivery service which I'll discuss in an upcoming chapter.

MONEY

If you were 'lucky' enough to have money on you when you were brought into prison then this will be put into your 'savings' account and an amount (usually £10.00 for Basic level, £15.50 for standard convicted prisoners and £25.00 for enhanced prisoners at the time of writing) is transferred to your "spends" account and the balance you have available to spend will be shown on the canteen kiosk screen or printed sheet. Prisoners on true remand are entitled to more if they have it in their savings account.

When you settled into the prison and are either working or are in education whatever you earn each week will also be added to your "spends" balance.

You can get money sent into you by family and friends. There is a method to send money in electronically using your bank as sending cash is unsafe and is to be discouraged and the only other way is either by sending a cheque or a postal order both of which are slower and can cost the sender in the case of Postal Orders.

Look at the internet website for your particular prison to see the correct address etc. Any cheque or postal order should be made payable to NOMS Agency and the name and prison number should be written on the back.

Whatever method is used to send you money be aware that it takes time to clear into your private cash account although the electronic transfer method is usually the fastest.

If you are being held at a private prison the methods of sending in money may be different so make sure you check before sending or having money sent in.

STAFF

As a new prisoner you'll typically only meet a few different types of staff over the first few days but let me tell you that as time goes by, you'll find out there's more and more of them, some you'll meet, some you won't but they're all there to make sure that the prison runs smoothly and is a safe and secure environment.

Let me break down the various staff into groups and subgroups for you:

- There are uniformed staff (operational) and these can be split into two subgroups; Prison Officers and Officer Support Grade. If you are being held in a private prison the names used may be different but the concept is the same.

Prison officers can be distinguished by the shoulder epaulettes they wear. A basic grade Officer has one stripe, a Supervising Officer has two stripes and a Custodial Manager has three stripes. Then there are the OSG's (Officer Support Grade) who don't have any stripes.

Above these are various levels of governors who are not in uniform but will have typically served in uniform before promotion and are still considered as 'operational'. Within any prison there may be many governors of various grades and specialities, such as security, residential, safety, operations etc who will typically report to the top governor usually described as "the No.1 Governor" although there will also normally be a deputy governor (the No.2) who may deal more with the day to day running of the establishment whilst the No.1 deals with the 'bigger picture' and the higher management within the Prison Service.

- **Secondly** there are administration staff who carry out all the administration duties required within the prison.
- **Thirdly** here are the "service providers" who work within the prison. These are typically not direct employees of the Prison Service, maybe being employed by a trust or charity (for alcohol or drug counselling or health clinics), an education provider for education classes or manual skills workshops running courses such as plumbing, plastering etc, healthcare providers provide nurses, and other limited medical care.
- **Fourthly** there is usually a maintenance team (who may or may not also run the warehouse (Stores) who are tasked with keeping the prison running on a physical level and their staff can include electricians, plumbers and decorators to name a few.
- **Finally** there are the members of the clergy, prisons almost always have a mult-faith chapel that can be used by Christians (C o E, Roman Catholic,etc) Muslims and other faiths that may be represented in the prison and there is usually a main chaplin who works with and manages the other religious personnel.

Whatever their status of job description these individuals can all have an impact on your time in prison.

Just try to remember, all of the staff are people as well and they, like you, have good days and bad days. Prison staff are dealing day-to-day with prisoners from all walks of life and with all types of issues and problems. Their main purpose is "to carry out the instructions of the courts, to ensure that society is protected and to make sure that prisoners are kept in a safe environment". In simple terms that means the staff are there to keep you from escaping and ensure that you are as safe as is possible, it does not mean that they are there to make you happy!

Most officers will face rudeness, hassle and hostility from some of the prisoners in their care on a daily basis; if you are reasonable and polite in your dealings with them you will find that they will actually do more to help you than those who are always complaining and being difficult, it's human nature. Just try to treat them as you would like to be treated yourself.

Unfortunately, just like there are always some prisoners who seem to enjoy being difficult, violent or who for some reason blame the officers for the fact that they're in prison, there are I'm afraid occasionally some prison officers that will treat prisoners with less respect or humanity than is ideal, or appear to be lazy and won't do anything to help you, but, during my years in the service I'm glad to say I've seen this type of officer become a lot less common, with the vast majority of officers nowadays being intelligent, considerate individuals who want to do the best for those under their care (prisoners) in a professional manner.

However, I would recommend that you bear the following in mind; officers rely heavily on the support of their colleagues and the sense of camaraderie is very strong, the closest parallel I can think of is that it's similar (but not as strong) as the camaraderie that soldiers feel for their fellow soldiers in their section or platoon. This means that if you're dealing with one of the few officers who is rude, lazy, incompetent or even violent then do not, I repeat, do not respond with violence yourself or anything that could be considered as such. Within seconds of any violence against an officer there will usually be three officers on the scene, within a minute there will be six and within 2 minutes (in every prison I've ever worked in) there will be between ten and thirty officers all attending the 'General Alarm' (see next chapter) and they will restrain anyone not following instructions immediately whilst putting everyone else behind their cell doors until the matter can be clarified. If you encounter an officer that mistreats you then make a written complaint, these things do get investigated and the chances are that if you're complaining legitimately then others will be or will have as well.

You will generally be called either Smith or Brown (in the way your school teachers may have in the past) or Mr Smith or Ms Brown by the prison staff, and you should generally address staff by their name such as Officer Green or Officer White if you know their last name. The prison staff usually do know your name, but for a new prisoner it is difficult to remember the names of the prison staff and therefore a lot of prisoners will call male uniformed staff "Guv", "Boss" or "Sir", and all female uniformed staff "Miss". Those who wear a suit usually respond if they are called "Guv" or "Ma'am"! First names are very rarely used by prison staff, and in the presence of prisoners they will even address their colleagues as either Officer White, Officer Green or maybe Ms White, Mr Green. If you are in the same location with the same officers for a long period of time then some officers may start to use your first name but even if you find out by accident an officers first name you should never use it.

Remember, the staff are there to do a job, they are not there to make friends and whilst good officers will be friendly, effective and professional they are people who have strict rules and guidance to follow and an officer you get on well with, will probably at sometime or another have to do things (search you, search your cell, tell you and your visitor to sit further apart, restrain you if necessary) or instruct you to do something (transfer to another prison, move cells, get back in your cell) for the security or safety of the prison, prisoners or staff that you aren't happy with.

When that happens you have three options, take it personally and make your life inside harder, be grown up about it and realise they're doing their job or don't come to prison in the first place.

ALARMS

(Emergency Situations)

There are typically two types of situations in a prison that result in an alarm being raised.

The first is a fire alarm and as a prisoner locked in a cell, hearing a fire alarm in your residential unit (and possibly seeing or smelling smoke) can be a scary situation. However, there really is no reason to be scared for the following reasons:

- The vast majority of prison residential units are built out of stone, brickwork or concrete and have very little flammable material in them
- Most fires are actually started by a prisoner in their locked cell (believe it or not) and due to a cells construction they are very slow to spread
- There are smoke alarms everywhere so fires are discovered very quickly
- There are multiple methods of extinguishing fires available on the unit
- The staff on the unit are trained regularly in the use of extinguishers, hoses and smoke hoods
- Upon a smoke detector being activated the local fire brigade is automatically notified as is every officer in the prison
- Staff are aware of evacuation procedures and carry out drills to ensure that if necessary prisoners can be moved from the affected area to a safe secure area

The second (and more common) alarm is what is normally referred to as a 'General Alarm' and is usually regarding incidents of violence, threatened violence or (rarely) what's known as 'incident at height' by staff and 'someone on the bars' by prisoners.

I'm going to talk about arson in the following chapter and violence a little later in this one but first I want to talk about the 'prisoner on the bars' situation.

The 'on the bars' / 'prisoner at height' incident starts when a prisoner (sometimes two) get it into their head that by climbing up to a 'high' point and refusing to come down they will force the prison (governors) to agree to their demands. What demands you might ask? I've personally heard the following:

- A Big Mac meal with a chocolate milkshake for the protestor and cheeseburgers for the rest of the prisoners on the residential unit.
- The No.1 Governor to publicly apologise for the prisoners requested phone numbers not being put on the phone system as quickly as the prisoner wanted.
- Air-conditioning units to be fitted because it was a really hot summer.
- The head of the Freemasons to admit that the prisoner was innocent.
- The Prime Minister (John Major) to grant him a pardon.
- Wives or partners to be allowed in over the Christmas period for conjugal visits (beds and a bottle of wine to be provided).

Let me be honest, I have seen these and other variations dozens of times over the years and they've all had the same end result: the prisoner comes down without their demand being successful and they then are subject to disciplinary measures and it will have an effect on their later stages of prison life and release.

Let me repeat that. The prisoners demands are NEVER met, even if it's something apparently simple or easily done. The prison governors will never agree to any demand made under threat, simple as that; and for the obvious reason that if they gave in once, then more prisoners would do it and it would cause more problems. As it is, most prisoners know that such tactics don't work and that it just causes problems for them, both with staff and other prisoners who resent having activities stopped whilst the protest is ongoing. However, occasionally someone will think they have a genuine reason for complaint that isn't being dealt with properly and in their frustration think that protesting in this manner will get it sorted. It won't, I guarantee it.

Now, going back to General Alarms; such an alarm may be raised by someone (staff or even a prisoner) pressing one of the alarm buttons situated around all areas of the prison (where prisoners have access), or by staff in the control room who are watching the CCTV from one of the many security cameras around the prison or by a member of staff either using the 'panic alarm' feature on their personal radio or calling through an alarm on their personal radio. Most staff still carry whistles to use to alert staff in an emergency of other means aren't available.

If an alarm button is used then this will normally cause an alarm to instantly sound in the area (and some prisons even have flashing lights) to immediately alert staff in that area but regardless of how an alarm is raised the control room will issue a general alarm alert over the radios, informing all uniformed staff of the location of the alarm.

Depending on the prison and their local operating policies this will usually result in predetermined officers (chosen at the start of the shift) leaving their current locations to attend the alarm without delay. If the alarm issue is not dealt with quickly, or if the officers on the scene or the staff in the Control Room deem it necessary then another alarm will be raised which will result in 'all available' officers leaving their locations to attend the scene.

When an alarm is raised it is very important that you listen to what the officers are telling you to do and that you follow their instructions without delay or question. Officers have set procedures to follow during alarm situations and if you try to argue with an officer, take your time or refuse to follow their instructions then you can find yourself being restrained or charged later as during an incident the officers don't have the time to deal with you in the usual polite manner they normally try to use with you.

I would strongly suggest that if a fight breaks out between prisoners that you get away from the fight, ideally returning to your cell if it's open or standing by it if your cell door is closed.

Getting involved is never a good idea if it is prisoners fighting amongst themselves.

If you see an officer being attacked then it is down to your conscience and common sense, personally I have been aided on a couple of occasions by prisoners and was very grateful but keep in mind it may not make you very popular with other prisoners (depending on the circumstances) and it's possible that when other officers arrive they may misunderstand the situation initially.

Finally of course I should mention medical emergencies and security emergencies both of which do of course happen from time to time but will rarely involve prisoners across the prison unless there is either a serious Security issue (in which case everyone will be locked in their cells until the matter is resolved) or the medical emergency is serious enough.

ARSON

Have you ever been in a fire? If not, have you at least stood a little too close to a bonfire or even a barbecue?

If you have then you'll know that being anywhere near an uncontrolled heat / smoke source is a bad idea, especially if you don't have an easy way to escape said heat / smoke. It's a fairly well known fact that typically people die from smoke inhalation before getting burned to death.

Personally I've been in a proper residential fire and I can tell you that it's not like the movies or TV portray it. First of all, forget about a little bit of wispy smoke (like a little bit of mist one morning), smoke is thick and you can't see further than the end of your arm. You can't breathe it in either, I used to be a smoker and at the time of the fire I was in I took one 'breath' and was choking, and for days later I was coughing up black phlegm.

So, you can't see, you can't breathe and somewhere there's a heat source (the fire) producing all the smoke, that if you get too close to it will burn you.

In every country around the world there's only one group of people who regularly put themselves in harms way by deliberately going towards fire and smoke; those people are known as firefighters and they're amongst the bravest people on the planet because they knowingly put themselves in danger to rescue others.

Unfortunately, there is a second group of people, at least here in the UK, that also put themselves in the way of fire and smoke.

I'm not talking about arsonists who usually have some psychological fascination or financial motive behind their firestarting.

I'm telling you, believe it or not, that for some reason, certain prisoners decide that although they're locked in a small cell, usually with windows that may only open a few inches at best, setting fire to a pillow, a book, or even their own clothes, is somehow a good idea.

Imagine that, you're trapped in the smallest room in your current home with no way out beyond someone on the other side of the door letting you out. Do you think it sounds like a good place to start a fire? If you are suicidal then the answer could be yes but beyond that it's surely got to be the height of stupidity.

Yet every day, across the UK there will be at least one, and quite often more than one, incident within a British prison where a prisoner, locked in a cell, decides to start a fire. Very rarely is it a genuine suicide attempt, most often it is the prisoners way of 'protesting' against the system or some part of the system.

Let me explain what happens when a prisoner starts a fire in their cell; this is the procedure that every prison officer must follow in the event of a cell fire, to act otherwise puts that officer at risk of disciplinary action against them upto and including having their employment terminated and possibly even facing manslaughter charges in the courts.

So, a fire is detected, either by the automatic smoke detection system or someone raising the alarm. An officer will move swiftly to the apparent cell that is on fire and if possible using the observation panel (a little reinforced window in the cell door) or by touching the door for signs of unusual warmth, confirm the alarm is genuine.
The officer (soon to be joined by other officers) will then do the following, locate smoke hoods and prepare them to be used when near the smoke, open the fire cupboard and start pulling out

the fire hose or 'mist' hose (depending on the age of the prison and refurbishments), pulling said hose to the cell door, hopefully by now one officer will have appeared with the inundation key which is a key that opens the inundation point in the cell door. The inundation point is a circular removable section (about the size of a jar lid) that can be removed with the use of a special key, allowing the nozzle of the fire hose to be inserted into the cell door, allowing water (or a fine mist) to be sprayed into the cell to put out the fire without the cell door being opened.

Once the nozzle is in the door then the officer will indicate for the system to be turned on and then the water / mist starts and hopefully the fire is extinguished fairly quickly.

However, the prison officers are not allowed to open the cell door until they are certain the fire has been extinguished, as opening the door whilst the fire is active could cause the fire to spread. As a result of this, partly due to the fact that the very limited visibility makes this difficult to confirm and the water hose whilst in the inundation point is not easy to aim the officer using the hose tends to err on the side of caution and typically try to get everything in that cell absolutely soaking wet thus ensuring the fire is out.

So, let's review this so far: a prisoner for reasons best known to himself decides to start a fire in a cell in which he is locked. Said fire is discovered (usually due to the smoke) and the prison officers attend to deal with the fire. Typically, from my experience, it will be between 5-15 minutes before the cell door is actually opened and officers in smoke hoods will enter to drag out the unconscious prisoner.

Why so long you might ask?

Well, it depends on various factors, sometimes prisoners barricade their cell door, attempt to block the inundation point, threaten staff that any officer coming in is going to have a fight on their hands, I've seen them all. Also sometimes prisoners who are a known risk to staff and are usually dealt with by officers wearing PPE (personal protection equipment) will start fires in order to have a chance of hurting staff.

Anyway, the fire brigade will arrive (automatically alerted by the system) and they will officially confirm the fire is out.

The prisoner will either be unconscious or suffering badly from smoke inhalation and will be attended to by either healthcare staff (if the prison has them) or will be taken to hospital (under officer escort) in an ambulance that will have also been automatically called.

Most, if not all of the prisoners belongings in the cell will have been damaged / ruined by either the fire, the smoke and or the water from extinguishing the fire. Also their neighbours will generally not be pleased with them as water and smoke are fairly adept at getting into other cells during the 'incident' and thus damaging others possessions.

The prisoner will be put on a charge for discipline and when fit and able will be dealt with accordingly; this could result in minor punishment such as stoppage of canteen for a period of time, it will lead to the loss of employment and it could lead to the prisoner facing criminal charges which could result in time being added to their sentence or a completely separate sentence. Also, technically the prisoner can be 'billed' for the cost of damage done to the cell, furniture, TV and anything else damaged in the fire.

Finally, the prisoner will definitely be categorised as a 'high' risk prisoner for CSRA (Cell Sharing Risk Assessment) purposes which means that they will be moved to a solitary cell and will not be allowed to share a cell. As discussed earlier, having a cell to yourself or sharing a cell can be a blessing or a curse but in all my years walking the landings I would say around 98% of prisoners wanted to share as it made time go easier, regardless of the negative aspects.

Even without the punishment, the ruined personal items, the inadvisability of irritating fellow prisoners and the near guarantee of solitary confinement I've never understood why someone would risk their health, and their life, by starting a fire in a room they're trapped in. Sadly people do die every year from doing this, most are accidental deaths, they were just protesting at something and the situation got out of hand.

If there's only one thing you take from this book above all else it has to be, don't start fires in your cell, you won't be pleased with the results.

CANTEEN

The canteen is the prison shop where you can buy different items, depending on how much money you have (and are allowed) to spend. When I was a lot younger the canteen was a physical place within the prison (or even several physical places) looking a little like the local corner shop (but smaller); however those days have now gone.

Depending on which prison you're in, you'll either be provided once a week with a printed order form that lists at the top your name and how much you can spend, you fill in the order form and then give it back (usually a day or two later) and then around 7-14 days later your order (hopefully) will turn up or if you're located in one of the prisons that's gone 'digital' you'll follow a similar process on an electronic touchpad (kiosk).

So, what can you order? From tinned tuna, worcestershire sauce, mars bars, orange squash, pot noodles, biscuits, duvets, pillow cases, stereos, Muslim prayer mats, the range is both diverse and generally reasonably priced. Whenever you've read in the news-papers about prisoners spending their days playing on their Play-station or Xbox it's always something the prisoner has had to pay for (and typically save for), the Prison Service does not pay for prisoners entertainment, in fact prisoners even have to pay 50p (at the time of writing) per week for their TV (typically a small 14") which has most, but not all, of the main freeview channels.

So, let's imagine you're about to order your canteen. Depending on your IEP level and conviction status (more about this in later chapters) you'll have a maximum amount you're allowed to spend (assuming you have the money). In this example we'll say it's £20 and so you order some pot noodles, several packets of biscuits, some BBQ sauce, tomato sauce, spicy sauce (got to try to give dinner some flavour), a bottle of orange squash, some Haribo, some shampoo and soap (yes the prison does give you some but you want better), some more tea and coffee, some tinned tuna and other assorted goodies to try to make your life a little more comfortable. You add it all up (or get someone to if maths isn't your best subject) and put your order in. From here your order (and everyone else's) will be collected and sent to the company responsible for the provision of 'canteen', which is currently DHL. They'll then process the order, and, believe it or not, some prison elsewhere will actually have prisoners filling the clear plastic bags that will contain the orders. Once your 'bag' containing your order has been filled (excluding any out of stock items) it will be sealed with a printout of what the bag contains and delivered to your prison, along with everyone else's.

THIS IS IMPORTANT.... On 'canteen' day, when you queue up (with your ID card) to collect your canteen, before you open the bag check the receipt (printout) in the bag with what you can see. Do this quickly while the DHL people are still there and if you can see a problem them get back in the queue and speak to them, highlighting the point that the receipt says the bag contains the chocolate Hobnobs you ordered but your UNOPENED bag clearly doesn't contain any such Hobnobs. There is no point, at all, in you going to your cell, ripping open the bag, then realising your chocolate Hobnobs are listed on the receipt but are not in the bag and expecting the DHL staff to take you at your word that the items were missing. Remember, you are in a prison, and whilst you may not be lying I'm afraid many of your fellow prisoners have done in the past and will do in the future, so the DHL staff won't believe you; and it won't be personal. However, if the bag is still sealed then they'll make a note on their documentation and you'll get a refund. Yes, I realise that it means you're not going to be able to have a choccy biscuit with your tea but it's not the fault of the

DHL staff in front of you, truth be told some prisoner 100 miles away who packed the bag either made a mistake or ate them while no-one was looking!

Don't forget, from the day you make your order, it's usually between 7-14 days until your order arrives. This can actually get a little confusing to start with as it means that you will probably have placed two orders before the first has even arrived. I've dealt with many prisoners who, shall we say got quite upset when their canteen arrived a few days after ordering minus what they'd ordered, quite forgetting that what had turned up was the order they'd put in 10 days earlier. After a few weeks, money allowing, you'll have a weekly canteen delivery every week as long as you remember to place your order.

One thing that you can't buy through the canteen is clothing, so let's have a look at the clothing aspect of prison life in the next chapter.

CLOTHING

The one thing that always amazed me was the different attitudes prisoners have towards clothing.

Some will wear the provided prison 'kit' comprising of t-shirts, sweatshirts, jogging / tracksuit bottoms and the provided underwear and plimsolls type footwear.

Then there are those who seem to treat prison as a fashion show, displaying the latest expensive trainers, tops and jeans, each item 'allegedly' costing hundreds of pounds, presumably worn to impress other prisoners with a display of their success and wealth. These prisoners always reminded me of lads I grew up with, living in run-down council flats whilst driving BMW's in expensive clobber just to impress those that didn't know them

I said 'allegedly' costing hundreds of pounds for the following reason; imagine that instead of going and paying full retail for the latest Fendi jeans or Nike trainers you pop down to the local market and buy a reasonably accurate imitation (fake) version for 10% (or thereabouts) of the genuine items cost. You might arrive at court dressed in your finest fake Hugo Boss suit, and despite what your solicitor had suggested was a vague possibility, the judgement comes down that you're guilty and you're going directly to prison.

You arrive at prison, still dressed in your finest fake outfit, the Reception officers (who haven't been trained to spot fake clothing) direct you to get undressed and changed into a lovely prison ensemble usually consisting of a grey t-shirt paired with grey tracksuit bottoms (not Nike) and a pair of plimsolls, reminding you of when you were at primary school doing sports and the clothes you came in get recorded as being what they appear to be.

The general rule is that for the first 2 weeks of custody you won't be able to wear your own clothes but different establishments do seem to operate on different rules sometimes and I have seen some establishments allow prisoners to wear their own clothes from day 1 and others make them wait for 4 weeks.

When you arrive at prison you may have brought with you some limited amounts of your own clothing, but probably will want some more. There are limits on the type and number of articles of clothing you can wear and these will be set out on a facilities list which you can get from the prison.

There is a nationally agreed list but different prisons do seem to set out their own rules, an average or typical list on how many clothing items you can have of one type is shown below.

- You can have 9 lower garments (trousers, skirts, jeans, tracksuit trousers and leggings). These should not be black, except for leggings.
- You can have up to 15 upper garments (sweatshirts, cardigans, shirts, t-shirts).
- Up to 3 pairs of footwear, normally not more than 2 pairs of trainers.

The rules specify that clothes can only be brought in to prison for you at specific times and manner. Some prisons will allow clothing to be brought in by relatives / friends in the first 4 weeks, some the first 2 weeks, and then every 6 months or 9 months or 12 months...if that sounds confusing it is because although prisons have set national policies the fact is that a lot of prisons seem to operate their own 'local' policy.

The best advice, ask the prison you are in or you are going to be visiting about their policy.

POSSESSIONS

(Volumetric Control)

A member of prison staff will make a list of everything you brought with you. You should be able to keep some things with you – this is called *'in possession'* property and is noted.

Under one of the Prison Service Instructions (referred to as PSI's) there is the following:

'Property held in possession by any prisoner must be limited to that which fits into two standard size volumetric control boxes and an 'out-size item' unless the Governor agrees, exceptionally, to a prisoner holding property in excess of that limit or it is an item which is exempt from volumetric restrictions.'

A property box measures 70cm x 55cm x 25cm. You can fill two of these.
Each prison has rules about what you can keep in your possession.

Some items are only permitted if you earn 'enhanced' level on the IEP scheme. You can also lose permission to have some items if you are reduced to 'basic' level.

Any property that you had with you when you arrived at prison that you are not allowed to have 'in possession' or that exceeds your allowance of a certain type of clothing or exceeds your volumetric control will be stored in "Prop" (short for Property which is a storage area in part of the prison). This property can either be 'released' to a family member or friend at your request or will stay with you in whichever prison you are located in.

Now, many prisons don't seem to operate the volumetric control anymore on a day to day basis. When I started most Governors were pretty strict on the policy and if a prisoners cell started to look a bit 'full' with possessions we'd check it with volumetric boxes. However, times change and nowadays the only time that the amount of possessions has becomes an issue is when the prisoner is moving either from one cell to another or being transferred to another prison.

If you're told to move this will involve you packing up all your possessions into (normally two) provided bags (usually quite thick transparent bin liner style bags) and this will include all your clothes, footwear, books, canteen purchases, etc... which may not sound like a lot but when someone has been in prison for even just a few months it can be amazing how much stuff they have if the prison doesn't practice volumetric controls. When moving between cells within the same prison it won't usually be a problem if the prisoner has 3 or 4 bags of possessions but problems can happen when a prisoner is being transferred to another prison.

When a prisoner is being transferred to another prisoner then it can become an issue because the prison transport will only have limited space and the number of prisoners and the volumetric allowance will have been calculated. Imagine if you and your friends or family are going on holiday and have ordered a taxi to take you to the airport and you've been told you can fit 1 suitcase each in the taxi. If one of you turns up with 3 suitcases then there's simply not going to be space. In the same way, if a prison transport is collecting 5 prisoners and has space set aside for 2 bags each plus some property not held in possession (in 'Prop') then when a prisoner has more than allowed it will usually mean that some things will not get put onto the transport and they will either be sent at a later date (hopefully) to the new prison or they'll be sent to Branston, which is the main storage area for the Prison Service. Either way, as a prisoner this is really the last thing you want to happen to your possessions, items being sent separately to other prisons or storage areas frequently result in these things disappearing for weeks, months or sometimes even being lost in the system.

My advice, if you're in prison, try to adopt a minimalist view towards possessions. Keep what you need, don't accumulate possessions, as the more you have then the more you can lose.

CATEGORIES & TRANSFERS

If you're remanded to prison before your trial, or if after pleading guilty but before sentencing, you'll be sent to a 'local' prison. This doesn't mean that it's necessary local for you, it will typically be local to the court that is dealing with you, although it could be a prison local to where you were arrested which could be miles away from the court that will deal with you.

So, if you're arrested in Southampton for a crime that took place in South London and remanded to custody then you're first experience of prison is likely to be at HMP Winchester but the first time you are taken to court at Croydon Crown Court or Southwark Crown Court (for example) then the chances are you'll end up after your first court appearance at a 'local' prison for those courts (so possibly HMP Wandsworth or HMP High Down).

It won't matter to the prison service or the courts that you live in the Southampton area and that by moving you to the London area makes it difficult for your relatives, friends or even legal visitors to reach you easily. Regardless of how many times you request, beg or implore, you will not be eligible to be transferred back to a more convenient prison until you have been sentenced. This isn't the government being awkward, it's practical that you be near the court dealing with your matter and it's much cheaper for the taxpayer if you only have to be driven 10 miles up the road (normally with a few others heading the same way) than being driven hundreds of miles as the only passenger.

Here's a tip. If you are going to commit a crime and get caught then it's much better for you if it all happens in your local area. You'll be arrested locally, it will be a local court (unless it's so serious it gets sent to The Old Bailey, also known more formally as The Central Criminal Court) and if remanded you'll more than likely be remanded to the local prison.

Once you have been sentenced there's a high probability that you'll be transferred to a prison that's more 'suitable'. This will depend on various factors, including the type of crime, the length of sentence, how long you have left to serve and your age. There are currently around 88 prisons dotted around England & Wales, and for adults over 21 they are either Category A (most serious crimes with a high risk to the public), Category B (a lesser risk to the public), Category C (even less risk to the public), Cat D (also known as Open) with (little to no risk to the public).

For women and young offenders there are simply 2 categories, Closed & Open.

Most, if not all, 'local' prisons are Category B, not specifically because the remand prisoners within them are truly 'B Cat' risks but because it is safer to keep them in more secure environments until they are properly categorised which is something that won't happen until they have been sentenced.

The only exception to this is potential Category A prisoners, or 'Pot Cat A's' as they're known inside. These will be individuals who have been remanded on murder, firearms, high profile cases that have been covered in the media or where it is believed that the remand prisoner has the means to arrange or carry out an escape, this could be a millionaire fraudster, a drugs baron or even an ex-soldier who's been taught escape and evasion techniques previously.

In these cases the prison Security team will assess the prisoner and either 'fail' him as a Cat A (in which case he stays at the 'local') which happens around 98% of the time, or they'll 'pass' and usually within 24 hours the prisoner will be moved to an A Category prison where the perceived risks can be minimised due to increased security.

88

So let's look at an example:

Despite living in Southampton, for some reason you decided to commit a crime in Manchester and you weren't very clever about it and you left your fingerprints at the scene. Three days later you're relaxing at home when the police knock on your door and arrest you. After a night in the police station you're taken to Southampton Magistrates Court who decide that the offence is too serious for them to deal with so they'll pass it up to a Crown Court to deal with, and they also feel you can't be trusted to turn up for future court appearances and therefore remand you to prison. You're taken from court to HMP Winchester, which is handy for people you know to visit you and you spend the next month or so there waiting for your first Crown Court appearance.

In the old days (anytime before 2010) it was a given that your first Crown Court appearance would be in person but nowadays there's an ever increasing likelihood that it will be by video link (it's like Skype or Apple Facetime in a sense but I'll explain that more later on) which means that you'll be taken to the video link suite within the prison, have a short conference with your solicitor / barrister and then the court case will begin, with you being informed of the charges and being asked for your plea.

It should be noted that it is not your choice as to whether you appear before the court in person or via video link. The court decides how they want to see you and the prison are informed.

If you say you're ill the prison medical staff will see you and declare you fit or unfit.

If you refuse for any other reason (or have been declared 'fit' and still refuse) then a prison officer will more than likely give you a 'direct order' which if you refuse will result in you being 'charged' which will end up with you losing some of the few so-called 'privileges' you enjoy in prison (like having a TV, time out of your cell, ability to order from the canteen, etc) and, depending on the judges instructions, there's a strong chance you'll be 'restrained' onto the transport (bus) which is never the most comfortable outcome.

Think about it this way, you wake up and decide that you don't fancy going to Crown court today. There will be at minimum the judge, two barristers, your solicitor, several court clerks, possibly the jury (12 of them) and probably a witness or two. That could easily be 18 or more people, all waiting for you to turn up, all who will be (possibly) inclined to think a little bit less of you because your actions (or lack of action) meant they had a wasted day if you didn't turn up. Courts, judges and legal teams have schedule's to try to keep to and jury's have their own lives they've been yanked out of which they desperately want to get home to, and make no mistake, you can try refusing every day, but you will end up being dealt with by the system, not once has a court case been dropped because the accused refused to come to court. All you'll do is irritate the jury who are going to decide if you're guilty (and whilst they should only judge you on the evidence presented, never forget that they are people who may find it hard to be 'generous' in their interpretation of the evidence if you've irritated them), and the judge who'll sentence you if you're found guilty.

Sorry, I wandered off the subject there a bit; don't misunderstand me, the last few bits about court are all true and useful but a little off the subject of transfers. So back to the example….

You live in Southampton, committed a crime in Manchester, got arrested and remanded in Southampton and ended up at HMP Winchester as it's the nearest 'Local' prison after the magistrates decided to send your case to the Crown Court. Now, because the offence took place in Manchester the Crown court that is given your case is one of Manchesters two Crown courts, neither of which are local to either Southampton or HMP Winchester, but are close to the scene of the crime, the police force that investigated it, the victim(s) and any witnesses.

After a period of time ranging anywhere from a couple of weeks to a few months (assuming that your first appearance was done by video link) your case is scheduled to begin. Hopefully your solicitor will have pre-warned you, if not then the first you may know about it will be a knock on your cell door around 6am by a prison officer telling you to pack your stuff and get ready for court.

This is important - Pack everything you have with you, there's a very good chance you won't be returning and if you want it then you need to take it with you.

Typically around 30-60 minutes later the officer will return to take you down to the Reception area, here you'll be asked to check all of your stored property, this is property you came to prison with that for one reason or another you weren't allowed or able to keep in possession and will include mobile phones, keys, clothing that's not allowed (various reasons) and possibly electronic items such as tablets, computers, etc. You won't be given these items back, but you will be asked to check that all of the items you 'checked in' with are present in the big sealed transparent bags as they'll be coming on your journey with you. It's also at this stage that if you have 'court clothes', a suit and tie, or at least some smart'ish clothes that you brought with you or friends / relatives dropped off you'll be able to get changed into them so that you can look like a fine upstanding member of the community and not a prisoner in the standard grey tracksuit bottoms and t-shirt when you are in court. Trust me, whilst appearance shouldn't matter, if you turn up in dirty stained prison clothes with a black eye and a 'wicked' haircut some people will make assumptions about you that they wouldn't have made if you'd turned up in a suit, looking clean and innocent.

People don't understand this but the whole Crown court system, and to a lesser degree magistrates courts as well, place a lot of value on appearances and respect.

I'm talking about respect for the court (as an institution), respect between the barristers and most importantly respect towards the judge.

There's going to be a whole chapter on respect.

Now, back to the matter of transfers.

You've been to court, you've either been found guilty or pled guilty and you've most likely been sentenced. If you've been sentenced to 12 months or less then it's fairly likely that you won't be transferred between prisons unless you're seriously far from your home address (release address) or if the Prison Service needs to move you for their own logistical reasons.

What many prisoners fail to grasp is that their stay in prison is not a situation where if they complain enough they can get moved to a nicer more 'convenient' prison. Despite what the newspapers may have you believe, prison is not a holiday camp, the prison officers are not holiday reps and if you don't like the food, the accommodation, the available activities or your fellow guests then don't book again!

Whilst the above is slightly tongue-in-cheek it never ceased to amaze me how many 'regular clients' once they were released then proceeded to behave in a way that was almost guaranteed to ensure they were checking in with us again, sometimes within weeks.

Anyway, for those sentenced to over 12 months a transfer becomes more than likely although it could easily be weeks or months before it happens, and just like with court appearances a prisoner will most often have little warning of an imminent transfer.

A prisoner may have requested a transfer to be nearer family or friends, or to be in an establishment that has the courses the prisoner needs to complete to be eligible for parole or for categorisation progression or simply to be in a more suitable category prison. They may have made the request several months ago or several days ago, they may be feeling 'settled' in the current prison and decide they don't want to leave, or they may even be in a prison that is convenient for friends or family (and despite the Prison Services stated intention of doing things to help maintain and strengthen family ties) they could be transferred to a prison a hundred miles away.

The reason for the lack of notice is typically two-fold, although there is a third reason that I'll touch on briefly to begin as it does sometimes occur.

1)   Urgent Situation - Occasionally the Prisoner Movement Unit (PMU) at Head Office will have an urgent need to move some prisoners from one location (or many) to make room for other prisoners. So for example, many London Local Cat B's including HMP Wandsworth and HMP High Down (to name but two) had to have additional space to make room for the large amount of people who had been remanded following the riots in London. This meant that some prisoners (who were sentenced) were moved from these prisons to further outlying prisons to make room. Another example would be when prisoners in HMP Birmingham rioted (or in prison language carried out a concerted indiscipline) and over a hundred prisoners were moved out from there and distributed to other prisons around the country, which I'm sure resulted in some prisoners in the receiving establishments being moved to make space.

2)   External Security - If a prisoner is told that they're being transferred to a particular prison on a particular day, then it would be possible for the prisoner to pass this information onto friends or family outside who could, theoretically, create a plan to maybe try to intercept the transport and possibly help an escape.

3)   Internal Security - A prisoner who is told to pack their belongings as they're being transferred within the hour has a very limited timeframe to pack their items, contact family

(who have little time to create an escape plan as in point 2) and, if they were so inclined, try to come up with a legitimate sounding reason why they shouldn't transfer.

Let me explain how a transfer typically proceeds.

- PMU inform the prison that on a certain date, usually between 3-10 days away the prison is to send a certain number of 'suitable' prisoners to another named prison.
- The person in administration responsible for dealing with transfers (called the OCA) will then consult their databases.
- These databases should allow them to quickly find prisoners who are 'suitable' (the right category type prisoner, possibly suitable location) and ideally have requested a transfer to that particular prison. Various checks will be carried out to ensure that the prisoners selected can be transferred to the prison and that there does not exist any good reason for the prisoner not to transfer.
- Once a number of prisoners have been selected (with a few potential spares as well) then the OCA will send to their counterpart at the receiving prison a basic file listing details of the prisoners they are proposing to transfer. The receiving OCA will check the files, ensuring that none of the proposed prisoners are prohibited from their establishment and that they meet the acceptance criteria (such as the right category, the remaining sentence length, home address, etc) before replying either in the affirmative or negative.
- The OCA will then check that all the relevant paperwork is up to date in the prisoners physical file and assuming all is good then they'll enter the relevant transfer details on the computer system.
- Every day (Sunday - Thursday) the Reception staff will print off the list of which prisoners are due to be transferred the following day, prepare their stored property, arrange for their valuables to be collected from the cashiers office and then produce a list for the wing or houseblock staff to work

off the next morning.

-     Transfers usually occur after the court transports have taken place which means that normally it's left to the officers who are unlocking in the morning to notify the selected prisoners. The conversation, in my experience, after saying something along the lines of "Morning Smith, pack your stuff, you're transferring to HMP Wherever today in about an hour, Reception will come and get you" often follows one of several paths.
  - ○   "Cheers Guv, that's great news"
  - ○   "Oh OK Guv, thanks"
  - ○   "I don't want to go there"
  - ○   "F#@k off, I'm not going"
  - ○   "I can't go there Guv, I' ve got problems with people there"
  - ○

Now, obviously the first two are fine, the third, fourth and fifth are responses that are not going to normally result in a happy ending for the prisoner.

The last 3 responses will (or should) result in the officer adopting a bit more of a 'legal' tone and stating "You are to pack your possessions to be ready for transfer to HMP Whereever, if you fail to do so you will be refusing a legal order and will be put on basic and/or placed on a charge".

The "I don't want to go there" prisoners will usually at this point give in, knowing that they can't fight the system and win.

The "F#@k off, I'm not going" prisoners will either give in or go completely over the top, either throwing things, trying to attack staff or even barricading themselves in their cell.

The "I can't go there Guv, I've got problems with people there" prisoners should be asked straight away who these 'people' are; they'll either say things like "John and Dave, I don't know their surnames", "Speedy and Slasher are their road names but I don't know their real names" or just "loads of people Guv, I don't know their names"; either way the OCA will have checked to make sure that any known non-associates are not at the proposed prison. (A quick word about non-associates, when you enter prison you'll be asked for the names of any people you believe are in prison anywhere that you have a problem with and that you shouldn't be located near (and why), you should also inform officers during your time in prison of any 'enemies' you make whilst in custody) or anybody from the outside that you think could appear in prison.

If a prisoner refuses to go for (as far as the prison is concerned) a non-legitimate reason then depending on the duty governor and staff resources one of the following two protocols will be followed:

1)   A 'team' will be 'kitted up', attend your location, place you under restraint and take you to the transport, using appropriate levels of force, dependant on your resistance. This will result in you arriving at your new prison without your personal belongings, probably a reduced IEP status and some bruises or soreness from resisting the officers.
2)   Your IEP will automatically be reverted to Basic so you'll lose your TV, some association time, your job and any other 'perks', you may also be placed on a charge for more serious punishment to be decided, and more than likely the OCA will make a note of your name and will at the earliest opportunity mark you for transfer to another prison, and will continue to do so until you've been transferred.

What's the lesson from this chapter? Always make sure you've advised the prison (staff) at the earliest opportunity of any reason why you believe you shouldn't be moved from your current establishment, this way the OCA will have had the chance to look into the factors and if legitimate then you won't be selected for transfer.

However, if there's no genuine reason for you not to transfer (and sadly a transfer making it harder for family or friends to visit isn't a legitimate reason) then you're best off packing your stuff and moving when and where you're told. Fighting the system may lead you to have the occasional victory but overall you will lose and if your aim is to get out of prison and back to your family and friends as quickly as possible then fighting the system won't aid that desire.

ADJUDICATIONS

Adjudications are when you have been 'placed' on a charge (charged with an offence) within the prison and you must now attend a hearing about the matter which is basically a mini-court case with a governor (or for very serious matters a real judge will act as an Independent Adjudicator) sitting as the judge.

The prison has 48 hours from the discovery of an offence taking place to provide you with a charge sheet (called a DIS1) written by the officer charging you, informing you that you are charged with the specific matter. This means that the offence could have taken place days or weeks ago but if it has only just been discovered they can and must charge you within 48 hours.

Once issued with the paperwork a prisoner will normally be scheduled to appear within 1 day (excluding weekends and public holidays) and the following will happen:

You will be taken from your residential unit and brought to the adjudication room and the adjudicating Governor or Independent Adjudicator will hear the evidence of the reporting officer read out by that officer (if the officer is available) from the charge sheet (DIS1), and then they will ask whether the accused prisoner (or their solicitor if one is present) accepts the statement as read out or wishes to question the officer about the evidence.

If the prisoner, solicitor or the adjudicator want to ask any questions then if the reporting officer is not present, or not available via a video link, the hearing will then be adjourned until the officer is available. If the prisoner does not wish to question a reporting officer who is not present the officer's written evidence in the notice of report will be accepted.

Other witnesses may be called in support of the charge, if the adjudicator agrees their evidence is relevant, and they may be questioned by the prisoner or the adjudicator. Written evidence may be accepted in the absence of the witness as above if the prisoner and adjudicator have no questions about it.

The adjudicator will ask the accused prisoner if they wish to offer a defence to the charge, whether by a written or oral statement, to explain their actions or comment on the evidence.

If the prisoner wishes to call witnesses the adjudicator should ask for an outline of the evidence they are expected to give. Witnesses on behalf of the prisoner should normally be allowed to give evidence, unless the adjudicator considers the evidence unlikely to be relevant, or that it will only confirm what has already been established as true.

After hearing all of the relevant evidence the adjudicator will consider whether the charge against the accused prisoner has been proved beyond reasonable doubt, and if it is not proved, will dismiss the charge.

If the charge is proved then the adjudicator will decide the level and length of punishment or may decide to pass the sentencing on to an independent adjudicator who as a judge has the capability of imposing more serious or longer punishments including adding extra days to an existing sentence.

Over the years I've attended many adjudications and I can tell you clearly that if you've been charged then as well as the officers testimony there's usually also CCTV or body worn video camera evidence or physical evidence that makes the process a relatively simple matter for the adjudicator to rule on. Invariably, just like in the real courts, if you've done something and been caught at it then the punishment is almost always reduced if you admit your guilt at the start of the adjudication, express regret for committing the offence and don't waste everyone's time.

That's not to say of course that you should admit to being guilty for something you didn't do, or point out if there's something wrong on the charge sheet (wrong name, prisoner number, date, etc) to get the charge thrown out but denying the facts when faced with them is pointless.

Of course, one thing to remember is that you're better off by not being involved in incidents or situations where you risk being charged in the first place. Even if you are charged ten times and 'beat the rap' every time it will still be on your record and won't look good when it comes to HDC, probation or consideration for Enhanced IEP status.

SMOKING AND DRUGS

It is illegal currently to smoke in any prison in the UK, and, unsurprisingly considering it is illegal in the outside community as well, the use of illegal drugs is also not allowed.

However, and you may have read this in various newspapers or seen it on the odd documentary, illegal drugs are unfortunately fairly common in most, if not all of Her Majesty's prisons. Ross Kemps recent 'taste' of spice at HMP Belmarsh unfortunately highlighted this.

The ban on smoking tobacco, be it proper cigarettes or rollups has simply meant that tobacco has become one more item to be smuggled in and sold on at a tremendous profit, which results in prisoners falling into debt which leads to either them or their loved ones on the outside being threatened or subjected to violence until the debt is repaid.

For the prisoners who act as dealers inside they've almost fallen into a win/win situation, they can sell their goods, be it tobacco, synthetic drugs (spice) or the genuine items themselves at prices undreamt of on the outside (prices are anywhere from 5 to 20 times the outside street price!) they have a consumer base that typically will have used drugs before, their customers typically aren't going anywhere and there's plenty of 'muscle' to hire as protection / enforcement. Even better, not only is it easy to force someone in debt to 'hold' the stash in their cell (and often mobile phones as well) resulting in any finds made by officers extremely difficult to link to the dealers, but even when caught red-handed the resulting punishment is often far less than would have been achieved had the offence taken place on the outside with the police, CPS and courts full involved.

In fact, the person who risks the most in the whole enterprise is the individual who brings the prohibited item / substance into the prison in the first place.

Be it drugs, mobile phones, tobacco, or various other illegal items regularly conveyed into prisons two things are without doubt true:

1)   Nobody does so by accident. There are signs everywhere in every prison I've ever worked in. Everybody entering the prison is subjected to at minimum a metal detector scan and often a rub-down search.
2)   People get caught every single day and many end up serving prison sentences themselves.

So why do people risk their own personal freedom, their reputation and everything in their lives to bring prohibited items into a prison?

Well, it seems to come down to MICE which is an acronym often used to explain the motives behind espionage / spying and stands for Money, Ideology, Compromise or Extortion.

Money is an obvious one, if a member of the public, or a member of staff, is offered a sum of money to bring a small package inside the prison, sadly some will.

Ideology covers beliefs, feelings, etc and in this situation could mean a loved one risking everything to 'help' someone inside. The number of partners or family members I've seen arrested over the years (including grandmothers) has amazed and saddened me.

Compromise or blackmail typically arises when a small error or lapse in judgement is compounded by someone being pressured to do something else or the first mistake will be made public.

There are increasingly more articles in the newspapers about female officers or other female members of staff having improper relationships with prisoners and then being blackmailed into bringing items into prison for them or the prisoners friends.

Extortion is partially covered by compromise but doesn't require any initial wrong-doing by the person who then brings illegal items in. They could be extorted to bring something into prison through threats (or actual acts) of violence against themselves or loved ones.

Obviously, once caught, the vast majority will claim they did it for any other reason than money and whilst it is undoubtedly true in some instances it's my personal belief that the vast majority will have been motivated by the money.

It is sad to say but I would estimate that at least 50% (and probably more) of all illicit items that are inside UK prisons have been brought in by corrupt staff, either uninformed or civilian. Every single prison I've worked in has had an excellent Security department who have all labored under the most trying conditions of budget and staffing restrictions to make their prison as secure as possible and all have consistently failed.

Any prison will have on a daily basis the following people going through the gates, from the outside to the inside; uniformed staff made up of Operational Support Grade (OSG's) and Prison Officers (three grades), Prison service civilian employed staff (administrators), Prison Governors (various grades of management) and external contracted staff that can include classroom teachers, trades instructors and possibly medical staff of various levels depending on the size of the establishment, external deliveries and tradespeople as well as visitors (both official like solicitors and personal such as friends and family) for the prisoners.

Obviously depending on the size of the establishment and the routine this can easily be in the smaller establishments around 50 people and in the larger ones over 300 people daily and many of these people (staff mainly) will be able to temporarily leave the prison for a cigarette break or lunch break, meaning that some staff may enter the same prison several times a day.

I have never worked in an 'A' Cat establishment so I can't comment on them but I've never worked in a 'B' or 'C' Cat establishment that had the Security resources to search every single member of staff, and their lunch / handbag / rucksack every single time they entered the prison.

Personally I have never worked in the Security departments of the establishments I worked in but having known quite well a few Security Governors they all willingly (if unhappily) admitted that staff corruption was their worst headache and only constant consistent searches and a massive increase in their resources would halt it, a situation they fear will never happen.

As one said to me almost ten years ago now, "When an officer starting out takes home less than £300 per week and someone offers him £2,000 per week to bring in a package no bigger than two rounds of sandwiches, well, there's always going to be some that say yes. Do we find them? Sometimes, sometimes with intelligence, sometimes with luck, but we know we often don't."

Working as an officer this was something that I never really managed to understand. When you're an officer and you're relying on your fellow officers to back you up, to be there if you need them, to help you enforce the rules within the prison, when prisoners typically outnumber you around 30 to 1, why would any officer do something that makes the prisoners inherently more dangerous.

Let me explain. First of all we have the drugs themselves. For at least the last 5 years the main problems have been synthetic drugs (commonly known as Spice), these are typically laboratory produced chemicals designed to simulate more commonly known 'natural' drugs such as cannabis. However, these originally started out as 'legal highs' and were even sold in shops on the High Street as due to their exact chemical compounds they fell outside of existing drug legislation. This meant that a clever chemist studied the exact chemical structure of cannabis (for example), made a synthetic version that was almost (but not quite) identical and then sold it. The authorities would eventually get around to testing it (normally after media interest) and they'd then ban it, the clever scientist would alter it again slightly, and so the game continued. Now multiply that clever scientist by a thousand and add in some "I read it on the internet" chemists and you have a over-supply of variations.

The trouble is that 'natural' cannabis has known effects and most users are aware of these potential effects and these synthetic versions do not have the same effects because they are chemically different.
So, while a cannabis user may typically feel relaxed, lethargic, chatty or get the 'munchies' someone on Spice could feel insanely angry, paranoid or simply lose consciousness (or close to as Ross Kemp discovered) and this means that someone on Spice becomes a threat to either those around them or themselves. As an officer you have a duty to get involved and if you see someone on Spice fighting with the strength of three men, self harming or fitting you have to put yourself at risk to resolve the situation.

This means that every single time anyone brings into prison a prohibited substance they are putting officers safety and general well being at risk; the punishments they receive when caught are, whilst generally severe, in my opinion not severe enough.

My advice, don't use drugs or even tobacco in prison, you don't know what you're paying for, you'll end up in debt which will cause you or your loved ones more grief and the chance to leave prison without any addictions has to be an opportunity to take advantage of.

E-SUITS

In Cat B and Cat C prisons you are allowed, normally within 2 weeks of arriving, to wear your own clothes, provided they don't fall into prohibited areas such as hoodies, black trousers or white shirts (hoodies because they can cover the head / hide identity and black trousers / whote shirts as these resemble officers uniforms). You can of course opt to wear prison issued grey tracksuit bottoms and a grey, or blue t-shirt or sweatshirt.

However, there is a third group of prisoners, those who have the option of what to wear removed, usually on a temporary basis, although I have seen a few prisoners spend years in this situation.

These prisoners are all deemed, for one reason or another, to be escape risks.

A prisoner may have tried to escape from lawful custody in a number of ways, some of them somewhat surprising. If a police officer restrains you in order to arrest you and you break free and run off, getting recaptured seconds or minutes later could count as escaping from lawful custody. Jumping from the dock in any court counts, obviously trying to break out (in any manner) from a prison will count but so potentially will being found in the wrong cell at lock-up. Talking about escaping will possibly do it and having a record of previous attempts will definitely do it.

Many prisoners may be considered an escape risk only whilst outside the prison, whilst attending (under escort) a hospital appointment, a funeral or another legitimate reason for a prisoner to be outside of the establishment.

Once the Security department has decided that a prisoner is an

escape risk the prisoner is then informed of the decision and provided with an e-suit (commonly referred to as a "Noddy suit")
which is an all in one jumpsuit of (usually) green and yellow harle-
quin pattern.

For those considered to be an escape risk only when outside
under escort, they will have to wear this suit as a condition of
attending the outside appointment, for those considered to be
an overall escape risk they will be given the e-suit first thing in
the morning (during unlock) and their 'normal' clothes removed,
and at lock-up (bang-up) in the late afternoon / evening they will
swap their e-suit back for their clothes.

Whilst some prisoners will seem to enjoy the temporary notori-
ety that wearing an e-suit may bring them in their little section
of the prison, for most prisoners it's an annoyance that they can't
wait to be rid of.

My advice, don't do anything that's going to lead to you wearing one, they're not cool and they look very hot in the summer
months!

O.M.U

The Offender Management Unit (or Custody as older officers and long term prisoners still often refer to it) is the main administration department within the prison.

This is the department that will receive and hold all the paperwork (and computer files) regarding every single prisoner in the establishment (and historical records for prisoners released from that establishment) and process all incoming information from the police, the courts, the probation services and any other official organisation.

It is this department that will be told by the court of your next appearance (if you are being held on remand) and they will work out your exact release date if sentenced whilst with them, so when the judge sentences you to 29 weeks they'll work out how long you spent on remand and your exact release day, bearing in mind that in all but the rarest of cases you'll actually be released from the establishment halfway through your sentence anyway (although our new Prime Minister is seeking to change this for some sentences).

This department will liaise with the probation department who will be 'supervising' you for the remaining half (or longer) of your sentence, and if you're lucky enough to be granted HDC (Home Detention Curfew) otherwise known as 'tag' then it will be the OMU that will process this paperwork and deal with the relevant parties to facilitate the equipment being installed in your approved address.

Prisoners used to (in theory at least) be allocated an Offender Supervisor (normally located in the OMU) who was a Supervising officer on detachment to the OMU who were supposed to keep in contact with their prisoners and ensure that all the relevant paperwork was completed in sufficient time. Unfortunately, especially during the last 7 years or so following budget and staff cuts the officers were very often cross-deployed back to residential wings to cover staff shortages which led to Offender Supervisors rarely able to complete the relevant duties.

The powers that be recently decided to revamp the system and introduce something called the Key Worker Scheme, which many officers (myself included) simply saw initially as a re-working of the 'personal officer' scheme that was scrapped around 10 years or so ago. However, by all accounts this new scheme is, at least initially, working well with each officer (depending on establishments) seeing between 4-6 prisoners every week for 15-20 minutes, acting as a point of contact for the prisoners between other departments and empowering the prisoners to do things for themselves where possible. Only time will tell if staffing resources will allow this new scheme to continue to flourish or if it will be quietly cancelled and replaced (or refreshed) in the future.

Different establishments have different OMU setups but they may also include the Public Protection department (they make sure that prisoners aren't able to contact victims or witnesses) or / and a team of probation staff who are sometimes based in the establishment.

I've never worked in the OMU but the ones I've had cause to enter have always been a hive of activity and whilst sometimes answers seem to come a bit slowly from them I'm sure they, just as with uniformed staff, are understaffed and under appreciated.

FIND A PRISONER

Any individual that is trying to locate someone they know (or believe) to be in one of Her Majesty's Prisons) can use the free Government Prisoner Location Service.

When this department receives the request they will then contact the specific prison where the prisoner is held and the prisoner must give their permission for their information to be shared. If the prisoner refuses contact or doesn't respond to the enquiry then their location will not be divulged to the enquirer.

To use the service email:

findaprisoner@justice.gov.uk

You must include:

- your name, or the organisation you represent
- your date of birth
- your address including postcode
- the name of the person you want to find
- the reason you want to find them - for example you're their solicitor, or a family member
- any other names they may have used
- their date of birth

If the prisoner agrees then you will be provided with their Prison number, the name of the prison and their location (cell and wing designation) which will enable you to either write to the prisoner or request permission to visit them.

VISITS

As a prisoner, being able to receive visits from family or friends is one of the few 'privileges' that makes prison life bearable and hopefully it helps to maintain family ties.

As a new prisoner you are entitled to a visit as soon as you are sent to prison.
Typically in most prisons it is the job of the visitor to arrange this although this can cause a problem occasionally as the visitor may not know which prison you have been sent to so may actually have to wait to be contacted by the prisoner before being able to apply. .

The number of visits, length of visits and other variables all seem to differ somewhat from prison to prison but there are some constants which include:

- Remand prisoners get more visits (as they're not convicted they're technically innocent)
- Enhanced prisoners under the IEP scheme should get more visits
- A visit will be of at least one hour in length
- You will be allowed to wear your own clothes (unless you're wearing an e-suit) but you will be expected at all times whilst in the visit area to wear an armband or coloured 'bib' over your top so that it is very easy for staff to distinguish between prisoners and visitors.
- Visits will normally be 'open' which means you can sit opposite your visitors, usually separated by a small table. If for security reasons (previous behaviour) you are not deemed currently suitable for 'open' visits you may instead be put on 'closed' visits which means you will be in a closed cu-

bicle with your visitors separated by a perspex / glass window with either a grill or intercom system to communicate through.

- All visitors have to provide approved ID and submit to being searched to enter the establishment; most if not all prisons also use biometrics, which in this case means fingerprints.
- All visits take place under video and personnel surveillance. This means there are CCTV cameras everywhere in the visits hall and there are prison officers patrolling the hall as well.

As to the rest of it, well different establishment procedures seem to vary but generally you'll be allowed visitors as follows:

- A convicted prisoner is allowed at least two 1-hour visits every 4 weeks.
- A prisoner on remand (waiting for their trial) is allowed three 1-hour visits a week.

Now remember that if you're on Judges remand then you're considered to be a convicted prisoner so you'll only be allowed the lesser amount of visits shown.

Visitors will need to book a visit through either a website booking system, an email system or possibly by calling a special telephone number for the particular prison, requesting a specific day (or choice of days) to visit, and usually indicating whether an am or pm visit is preferred.

Once again, because different prisons have different situations it's not possible here to list all the variations but prisons will usually have at least one day during the week that visits do not take place, specific rules about how far in advance visitors must arrive to book in, have their ID checked and be searched. Similarly the length of visits may vary from prison to prison but the absolute minimum amount of time a prisoner and their visitors should be in the visit area together is one hour.

There will normally be a booth and or vending machines that will enable your visitors to buy delicacies ranging from hot or cold drinks, sandwiches, chocolate bars and crisps that they can share with you but let me give you a few bits of advice.

Sometimes the queue can be quite long at the start of the visit session, I have literally seen visitors spend almost half their allocated visit time standing in the queue to buy some tea and crisps whilst the prisoner sits (sometimes patiently) waiting for them as the prisoners aren't allowed away from their designated seating. My advice, try to balance the need for refreshments against the amount of allocated time you have together.

The next bit of advice follows on from this, there's no point in getting a partner, parent, friend or another visitor to buy you 10 chocolate bars so you can eat 1 and have 9 to take back to your cell because prisoners aren't allowed to take anything back with them from a visit. So unless you want to eat them all there and then there's really no point.

Final piece of advice for visitors and prisoners alike. Using the visit to try to 'smuggle' contraband (drugs, mobile phones, tobacco or anything else prohibited) into the prison will have one of three results:

1. The contraband will be discovered during the search process and the visitor will be detained until the police arrive and then arrested, charged and normally convicted (due to the video evidence combined with the officers statement and the actual physical evidence) which will result in a criminal record, a ban on visiting and in more serious (or repeat) offences a prison sentence of their own. In this case the prisoner will almost

always deny any knowledge of their visitors actions to the prison authorities.

2. The contraband isn't discovered when the visitors and their belongings are searched (this time but it really is just a numbers game) and they make / attempt to pass the contraband sometime during the visit. Most people when breaking the law are nervous about it and the officers patrolling the visits area and the CCTV operators recognise these signs and are also well versed in spotting the other signs that indicate a visit is not just a visit. Dropping items into drinks or crisp bags, passing things by mouth or hand, there's a great chance they'll be seen or recorded and staff will immediately intervene, removing the visitor, removing the prisoner (and quite often having to restrain the prisoner as they don't like to see their partner, parent or friend detained in front of them) and securing the items passed to be used later as evidence. In this case the visitor will go through the process as shown in (1) above and the prisoner will also face internal prison discipline and the possibility of criminal prosecution which could lead to another prison sentence.

3. The visitor successfully smuggles in and passes the contraband to the prisoner without detection. For the visitor it is very unlikely this will be a one time deal, as either pressure from the prisoner, other prisoners putting pressure on the prisoner or friends of other prisoners putting pressure on the visitor out in the real world mean that another delivery will almost certainly be attempted and once again this is where (1) or (2) shown earlier can happen.

This isn't even touching on the moral or commonsense aspects of smuggling contraband into a prison.

There is no legitimate reason to have a mobile phone in prison as every prisoner has the ability to use prison phones to contact people they are allowed to, with many prisons now having cells which actually have phones inside, as opposed to a few phones in the wings general areas. Mobile phones inside prisons are generally only used to facilitate (arrange) criminal activity, either inside or outside the prison. The argument that prison calls are too expensive isn't valid as the cost of smuggling a phone inside a prison and the risks around the smuggling make the argument ridiculous.

Drugs are obviously illegal outside so it's no surprise they're also illegal inside prison but as mentioned earlier, the super-inflated price of drugs, the debt and the ensuing violence all contribute in a very negative way to life inside, not just for prisoners but also the staff, and for the prisoners (and their loved ones) when upon released they have a drug habit or debt that needs repaying.

Visitors who bring contraband in will ultimately get caught or contribute negatively to the lives of those that they are visiting and 'helping'. Every year I've seen detection improve due to technological advances and staff training, and every year I see more and more visitors getting caught.

My advice, don't ask your visitor to do it and if you're a visitor being asked, consider this, does the prisoner asking really have your best interests in mind?

VULNERABLE PRISONERS

Practically every prison will have a Vulnerable Prisoner area which has the prisoners located within it separated from the other prisoners within the establishment.

These prisoners are separated for their own safety and for the good running of the establishment. What this means is that it has been decided (usually due to previous incidents) that having this particular prisoner in with the 'general population' could lead to the prisoner being in danger of physical harm, which in turn could lead to staff having to deal with violence that would put prisoners and staff at risk of physical harm and disrupt the smooth running of the prison.

There is a misconception about prisoners who are in the VP unit (as it is most commonly known) which whilst not completely inaccurate is not 100% accurate.

The prisoners who are usually housed in a VP unit will usually include; sex offenders (of all types), ex police officers, ex prison staff, ex magistrates or judges, prisoners who are famous (either due to their crime or their previous life, ie, pop stars, actors etc...), prisoners over 70 (depending on the prison), prisoners who due to their personalities are deemed to be especially vulnerable due to bullying) and anyone else that the prison staff deems could be at risk if they were housed with the general population.

In a prison there is a hierarchy, if you like it's almost a class system. Some criminals (or crimes) will be considered to be more 'acceptable' than others, for example, when I started in prisons the bank robber was of a higher standing than a burglar who was higher than a mugger who was higher than a street drug dealer and so on. Things have changed a little (as have some crimes) but the one constant has been that sex offenders have always been at the bottom of the hierarchy.

In fact, even amongst sex offenders there's a hierarchy although it tends to be a little more difficult to understand but it goes along the lines of people convicted of indecent exposure or indecent assault look down at rapists who look down on people convicted of indecent acts with children who look down at people convicted of indecent acts with animals.

Add into the mix a couple of ex-police, prison staff, judiciary or others convicted of non-sexual offences but housed with the sex offenders for their own safety (for some reason ex police, prison staff and the judiciary are never very popular with ordinary prisoners) who generally feel a level of revulsion or disgust at having to share their accommodation with sex offenders and you have a fairly typical vulnerable prisoners unit.

VP prisoners are not only housed separately, they are also normally segregated from other prisoners in work and education areas and during movements around the prison. The only occasions that VP's may typically be in the same area as other prisoners is during visits (although some establishments do still separate them) and also in religious services.

Being under Rule 45 (the prison rule related to VP's being segregated for their own safety) is a largely voluntary state of affairs, prisoners who meet the criteria will be offered the choice of 'accepting the rule' or going into normal population, usually after having been advised of the general prisoner population reaction / feeling to prisoners with similar offences. Most will accept, some will not and will simply hope that by lying to the other prisoners about their offences (or alleged offences) they'll be able to live amongst the general population; although nowadays when smartphones are regularly found in prisoners cells it doesn't take more than a few minutes searching on Google to find local news reports so those people are risking their safety in my opinion.

Then there are the prisoners who don't consider themselves to be sex offenders. Consider a drug dealer sentenced to three years for possession with the intent to supply, who was also convicted of rape or indecent assault and sentenced independently for that but he doesn't consider himself a sex offender because the rape or assault was either to do with an underage girl who was 'available' to gang members or the rape was just part of a gang initiation so 'it doesn't really count'. Previously, the vast majority of those prisoners wouldn't take the rule, kept the sex aspect silent and claimed to be inside just on the drugs charge but recently I've noticed in a couple of prisons that some of these individuals are now choosing to live on the VP unit, not because they have something to fear but because the VP unit is full of individuals that might be more susceptible to bullying, threats of violence or other undesireable outcomes.

This in turn has led to the VP units slowly changing from places where the vast majority of the inmates are amongst the most compliant, non-violent prisoners within the prison to a place where sudden bursts of violence are unsurprising and the attitude of prisoners towards staff and the rules has taken a sharp downturn.

I.E.P - INCENTIVE & EARNED PRIVILEGES

Each prison has an Incentives and Earned Privileges Scheme. This is usually shortened to 'IEP'.

Prison staff will tell you which IEP level you are on and if it changes. Your IEP level will say if there are extra things you can get or do.

Your IEP level depends on whether you:

- keep to the rules
- take part in work and other activities
- show a commitment to your rehabilitation
- help other prisoners or staff

For example, if you follow the rules and do good things for yourself in prison you may be able to do things like:

- spend more of your money
- get more visits from your family and friends
- earn more money
- have a TV in your cell
- wear your own clothes
- spend more time outside of your cell.

You can also have these things taken away from you if you do not follow the rules.

The extra things you can have or do are different in each prison as the management (Governors) have some level of control in this area).

There are now three IEP levels as the 'Entry level' has been recently removed.

The following is a general guide as to what they mean as the new Incentives Policy Framework (PF) has recently been published. This new policy gives Governors some discretion to design a local incentives policy providing they adhere to some requirements. Prisons are expected to have local policies in place by 13 January 2020, though there are some things that should have happened before that – for example on 16 August 2019 all prisons should have stopped using the 'Entry level', with prisoners automatically starting on 'Standard level' and from 27 September 2019 all prisons should all have 'Incentive Forums' in place.

Basic level

If your behavior has been poor (which can include rudeness to staff, failure to follow instructions, etc) you will be put on 'Basic' level.

If you are on 'Basic' level it means you can only have certain things that the law says you must have, like some letters and visits. You will not be allowed anything extra like a TV, extra association time out of your cell and some prisons will remove your personal clothing forcing you to wear prison issued clothing.

Standard level

Upon entry into the prison system you will be put on this level and will remain on this level by taking part in prison activities, showing a commitment to your rehabilitation and behaving well. The majority of prisoners serve most of their sentences on this level.

Enhanced level

If you can show that you are committed to your rehabilitation, take part in work or education and other activities, and follow prison rules for at least 3 months, you may be considered for 'Enhanced' level.

You also need to show that, where possible, you have helped other prisoners or staff. For example, by being a Listener (Samaritan trained counsellors) or Peer (a prisoner with special responsibilities usually involved in helping prisoners with specific problems).

If you are transferred to another prison you should keep the IEP level that you had before unless you are transferred due to poor / violent behaviour in which case your IEP level may have changed just before you moved.

Be aware that the IEP scheme at the receiving prison may differ in some ways which could affect your IEP level at a later review although it would be quite unusual for this to happen; what is more likely is for an 'Enhanced level' prisoner to discover that their new prison does (or does not) allow something their previous prison did.

If prison staff think you have behaved badly they may give you an 'IEP warning'. This may be for failing to follow staff instructions or behaving in an unacceptable manner but the member of staff has decided to 'warn' you rather than immediately 'punish' you. If you get an IEP warning, prison staff must decide how long it stands for. This should not be more than 12 months. If you get another IEP warning in the active timeframe then prison staff will review your IEP level. This means they could change it to a lower level.

If you are on Basic level this should be reviewed after the first 7 days and then at least every 28 days after that but normally every 7 days.

If you are on Standard level you can apply for Enhanced after 3 months. If you do not get it, you can apply again every 3 months. Otherwise, your IEP level should be reviewed once per year.

If you are on Enhanced level this should be reviewed once per year.

Your IEP level can also be reviewed at any time if you receive two IEP warning or something serious happens and the prison thinks your IEP level may need to change.

The IEP scheme is not part of the disciplinary system and so is separate to the adjudications process.

If the prison thinks there is good reason to, they can decide to give you an adjudication as well as review your IEP level.

If you have been put on basic for an incident that you are later found innocent of at adjudication, you may want to appeal your IEP level through the complaints procedure if the matter isn't corrected by a Supervising Officer or Custody Manager on your residential unit.

Decisions about your IEP level should be 'open, fair and consistent'

If you think you have been given an IEP level or IEP warning unfairly, you can make a complaint using the internal complaints process.

One thing to be aware of is that in every prison I've worked in the 'Enhanced level' has been unavailable to prisoners on remand or appealing their conviction for the reason that to qualify for 'Enhanced' a prisoner needs to be actively engaged in their sentence plan as a commitment to their rehabilitation, which means attending courses designed to address their behaviour that led to their imprisonment to reduce the likelihood of them reoffending.

If you're a prisoner who is either on remand and therefore not convicted, or a prisoner going through the appeals process to get your conviction overturned then 99% of the time you won't be engaging with your sentence plan as you won't have one (remand prisoners) or you'll feel that attending courses to address your offending could undermine the fact that you're claiming you didn't offend (appeal prisoners). However, if you do fall into one of these categories it is still advantageous for you to interact as positively with the prison staff and services as it will make your life easier whilst inside.

If you apply after 3 months for 'Enhanced' and are successful then depending on the prison you may get more visits (or longer visits), possibly more gym time or time out of your cell for 'association' and other benefits including an increase in the amount of money you can spend within the prison each week (assuming you have the funds available) as well as other 'advantages' dependant on the prison you are in.

If you apply and are not successful for some reason then politely ask why and actually listen to the answer, this allows you to work on the issue and then when you reapply in 3 months time hopefully you'll be successful.

Another thing to keep in mind is that individual prison officers have a degree of choice they can use when dealing with matters. They can issue you "warnings" about your behaviour which are simple verbal warnings and not noted on your records, they can issue you with a 'negative' or 'red' entry on the computer system which will remain on your record but will only be taken into account when staff are considering 'Enhanced' applications, 'HDC' applications or looking for some other reason to assess your general behaviour within the prison environment or they can formally charge you (give you a "nicking") where the issue is felt to be serious enough that it requires an adjudication before a governor and this will be noted on your records. If the charge is proved then the adjudicating governor will either decide on a suitable punishment which could be cellular confinement (more time in cell, less time outside of cell for a period), loss of canteen (not able to buy goods for a set period of time), reductions in visits etc. If the offence is deemed serious enough the prison may pass the case to a visiting judge (independent adjudicator) who will decide what sanctions are appropriate and this can include additional time being added to your sentence.

In some cases, usually to do with assaults against staff (or serious assaults against a fellow prisoner) or finds of large amounts of drugs then the matter will be dealt with by the police and CPS and prosecuted as a separate offence with separate sentencing.

COMPLAINTS

As a prisoner you have the right to complain if you think that you are being treated unfairly or if something has happened that you feel is cause for a legitimate complaint.

The thing to remember about making a complaint is to be polite and accurate about it. Shouting at an officer to complain will not result in a happy ending, complaining under your breath will not result in your complaint being looked at and being vague will mean that the complaint is generally not dealt with as quickly as possible. Always try to speak politely to officers, you'll generally get better results; just remember officers are not your servants.

The prison system has set procedures for complaints, which should be followed to ensure that you have the best chance of your complaint being resolved.

First of all, consider what you are complaining about; are you complaining about something outside the prisons control, like your court case taking too long, the police not contacting you, your partner not visiting you, the judge sentencing you to longer than you expected; these are things the prison can't control so you're wasting your time complaining to the prison about them.

Secondly, if it is a prison matter, is it relevant to your residential unit, like a lightbulb not working in your cell, the toilet being blocked, not being unlocked when you should be, noisy prisoners keeping you awake, not enough mash potato with your dinner, etc... if so then politely speak to the officers that work on your residential unit, making a note of who you spoke to and when, if it isn't dealt with reasonably quickly then try again or try to speak to a Supervising Officer before filling in a Complaint form.

If you feel it's a legitimate complaint and it can't be (or hasn't been) handled by the staff on your residential unit then you need to complete a Complaints form that will (should) be available on every residential unit.

Make sure that you use the right form as there are several forms, one is the Complaint form, one is the form for appealing a decision regarding a complaint (when you don't agree with the complaint reply), there's a form for complaining directly to the main governor (No.1 Governor) and a form for contacting the IMB (more on them later) and if you use the wrong form it can result in your complaint not being dealt with quickly or indeed it may be sent back to you saying it needs to be on the right form.

Fill in the form carefully, you will need to put your name, prison number, cell location and signature on the form as well as clearly stating why you are complaining and what you want to happen regarding your complaint. If you have spoken to staff about this then name them if possible, try to use dates where applicable and do not use threatening or rude language.

Once you have completed the form you should place it in the specific complaints box provided on the residential unit where it will be collected by a member of staff and passed to the relevant department. They will make a record of your complaint and send it to a senior member of staff that is judged to be most likely able to answer / resolve the complaint. You should (may) receive a letter back confirming that the complaint is being looked at and you should get a complete answer within a few weeks typically.

If you have put a complaint in then there is no point sending in another complaint about the same thing, time after time, every day or so as you are simply generating more paperwork and actually slowing down the process so your reply will be delayed.

When you get a reply it will either ask you for more information, it may say your complaint is refused because the facts available do not support your complaint or your complaint is agreed with and a solution will be proposed.

If your complaint was refused then you can appeal against the decision within a certain time frame of receiving the refusal. You need to fill in the appeal complaint form, stating which complaint you are referring to and why you are appealing against the previous decision. This will be dealt with by someone senior to the original complaint responder and you need to be factual and accurate in an appeal; appealing by saying the decision was wrong isn't enough, you need to say why you believe it to be wrong and provide or suggest evidence that could exist to support your complaint. If the appeal is rejected then you have no further appeal rights within the prison but you can write to the Prison Ombudsman but this is a lengthy process and should only be considered for the most serious of complaints.

You can also complain to the IMB but in this case no member of prison staff will see the complaint or the answer and in most cases even if the IMB agree with your complaint it won't actually solve the issue.

Another option is to write a 'Confidential Complaint' directly to the No.1 Governor, sealing it in an envelope before placing it in the post box. When collected this will be taken to the Governor's office where it will be looked at when the governor is available to do so. Many of these complaints should and could have been dealt with as ordinary complaints and if the Governor reads the complaint and feels it is not a confidential complaint matter they should have it returned to the prisoner with the suggestion that it be written out on a standard complaint form, thereby delaying the whole process for around a week. If the Governor decides the matter is of a confidential matter then they will either investigate the matter themselves or more likely pass the matter to a lower grade Governor responsible for the area or aspect of the complaint. When the confidential complaint is answered the response will be in a sealed envelope.

INDEPENDENT MONITORING BOARD (IMB)

This is a group of unpaid volunteers, normally made up of people who may have had careers in the law, charitable organisations, business or education that voluntarily spend some of their free time in prisons across the country.

Their purpose is to be an independent group, outside the Prison Service (or government) control who monitor that prisons are run correctly, with an emphasis on prisoners being dealt with safely and fairly. It is actually a little known fact that they are also there to ensure prison staff are treated fairly, sadly the general feeling amongst most uniform staff is that the IMB always take the prisoners side in a dispute and are unfairly biased towards the prisoners viewpoint.

Having dealt with the IMB on several occasions I can tell you that in my experience they are on the whole completely unbiased and very fair; sometimes they ask questions which uniformed staff don't like but that's normally because local policies in operation in a particular prison don't always match official national policies which the IMB will refer to.

However, having said that, a prisoner complaining to the IMB for the initial complaint, or even instead of an appeal is really wasting their time, by their very nature all IMB complaints are confidential so the complaint matter won't be raised or resolved with staff. Having had informal conversations with IMB members I understand that the vast majority of the complaints they receive are either about complaints not being dealt with fast enough or complaining about staff behaviour towards them, both matters the IMB can not do anything about.

HOME DETENTION CURFEW

(HDC)

Some prisoners can be released early subject to a curfew which requires them to be at home between certain hours per day (usually from 7pm in the evening to 7am in the morning), allowing them to live at home and work during the final weeks of their sentence. They are "tagged" with a small device which is fitted to the ankle or wrist. The tag sends a regular signal to a device located in their home that connects to a monitoring centre which confirms the presence of the person in their place of curfew. If they are absent or try to tamper with the equipment (like cutting the tag off and leaving it at home while going out) the monitoring centre is alerted and the breach investigated, usually by the monitoring company or the local police.

Someone in prison may be eligible for HDC depending on things like their sentence length, current and previous offences and their behaviour during this and previous sentences.

Someone will not be eligible for HDC if any of the following apply:

- they are serving 4 years or more for any offence;
- they have been convicted of a sexual offence and are required to register;
- they are currently serving an extended sentence for violent or sexual offences;
- they are serving a sentence for failing to return on ROTL, absconding or escape;
- they are serving a sentence for breach of the curfew require-

ment of a Community Order

- they have ever been recalled to prison for failing to comply with HDC curfew conditions;
- they have ever been returned to custody by the court for committing an imprisonable offence during an 'at-risk period' of a previous sentence.
- they are currently serving a recall from early release on compassionate grounds;
- they are a foreign national who has been recommended for deportation by the court or they are liable to deportation and a decision to deport has been served.

Even when potentially eligible there are a number of reasons they could be 'presumed unsuitable' which can include:

- anyone with a history of sexual offending but not required to register;
- foreign national people with convictions liable to deportation but not yet served with a decision to deport or an immigration hold notice
- anyone who has been recalled for poor behaviour during a previous period of HDC

Also, anyone serving a sentence for any of the following categories of offence is usually 'presumed unsuitable':

- Murder
- Explosives
- Possession of an offensive weapon
- Possession of firearms with intent
- Cruelty to Children
- Racially aggravated offences
- Terrorism

The minimum amount of time HDC lasts is 14 days with a maximum of 3 months for those serving less than 12 months, and a maximum of 4 and a half months for those serving 12 months to 4 years.

Those serving between 3 and 4 months become eligible for HDC after 1 month in custody. Those serving 4 to 8 months become eligible after serving a quarter of their sentence and those serving more than 8 months and less than 4 years become eligible 4 and a half months before their automatic or conditional release date. Time spent on remand counts towards eligibility.

Before HDC can be granted the prisoner has to undergo a risk assessment and interview which will involve the prison, the probation service and the police, and sometimes doctors, social services and victims. It will take into account their prison record / behaviour, previous convictions and the suitability of their home address. If HDC is refused, the person will be told this and given the reasons why.

The probation service on the outside will be asked to check the address the prisoner has given, and this will form part of the risk assessment. They may want to visit the family to assess the effect HDC might have on them and to ensure that everyone living at the address is aware of all the implications of having someone on HDC living there.

The duration of the curfew must be spent at the same address. This can only be changed in exceptional circumstances and at the discretion of the Governor. Any new address will be subject to the same checks and the person may not move in until it has been approved.

One-off absences can be granted in special circumstances subject to prior approval. These can include:

- Attending a wedding or funeral of a close relative
- Unexpected medical appointments / operations
- Job interviews or attendance at job club or benefit office
- Attendance at court as a witness or defendant

The person will have to provide proof of the reason for their absence.

Regular events such as attending a place of worship, shift work or education can be accommodated and should be taken into account when the curfew hours are initially set.

Within the prison it will be OMU staff that are dealing with the paperwork for the initial HDC assessment and processing other information, a process that apparently starts around 4-6 weeks before the HDC date, thereby ensuring the information and decision has been received by the HDC date whenever possible.

LICENCE (PAROLE) & RECALL

Most prisoners in prison are there on determinate (fixed) sentences and will be released at the half-way point of their sentence and will spend the remaining months or years of their sentence 'on licence'. Being released on licence allows the prisoner to reintegrate into the community, rebuild family ties and helps to prevent re-offending (or that's the idea behind it anyway).

Being released 'on licence' means that for the rest of the sentence (imposed by the court) the released prisoner must stick to certain conditions. Time spent 'on licence' in the community is supervised by the Probation Service.

Before release from prison the prisoner will be given the licence and have the conditions explained, copies of the licence will also be kept by the prison as well as being sent to the probation supervisor. Copies will also be sent to the local Police force in the area where the prisoner will live and to the National Identification Service at the Metropolitan Police.

The prisoner being released will also have it explained to them during the prison release process that they are expected to attend an appointment with their probation officer, usually the same day of their release or the next day. Sadly, a small percentage of prisoners fail to even manage this and are recalled back to prison within 24 hours of leaving.

The paper licence received by the prisoner will include the seven standard conditions set out below as well as any extra conditions that the Offender Manager has decided are relevant and necessary to enable progress and prevent reoffending.

As I said above, the prison staff should fully explain all of the licence conditions before release. If the licence conditions are broken the prisoner may be sent back to prison.

The seven standard licence conditions for prisoners serving determinate sentences are:

(a) be of good behaviour and not behave in a way which undermines the purpose of the licence period
(b) not commit any offence
(c) keep in touch with the supervising officer in accordance with instructions given by the supervising officer
(d) receive visits from the supervising officer in accordance with instructions given by the supervising officer
(e) reside permanently at an address approved by the supervising officer and obtain the prior permission of the supervising officer for any stay of one or more nights at a different address
(f) not undertake work, or a particular type of work, unless it is approved by the supervising officer and notify the supervising officer in advance of any proposal to undertake work or a particular type of work
(g) not travel outside the United Kingdom, the Channel Islands or the Isle of Man except with the prior permission of your supervising officer or for the purposes of immigration deportation or removal.

(*Source: Ministry of Justice – PSI 12/2015*)

Extra conditions may also be imposed under one or more of the following categories:

(1)   residence at a specified place
(2)   restriction of residency
(3)   making or maintaining contact with a specific named person
(4)   participation in, or co-operation with, a programme or set of activities

(5)	possession, ownership, control or inspection of specified items or documents

(6)	disclosure of information

(7)	curfew arrangement

(8)	freedom of movement

(9)	supervision in the community by the supervising officer, or other responsible officer, or organisation

If a person on licence breaks any of the conditions of their licence they can be recalled to prison immediately, or, depending on the circumstances (usually minor), receive a warning the first or second time they break the conditions of their licence. If recalled to prison it will be for either 14 days, 28 days, for the remainder of your sentence or until the matter is heard by the Parole Board.

How long a person remains on licence depends on the length of the sentence, the age at conviction and the date of conviction as different rules and laws came into effect at different times. This will be stated in the licence.

RELEASE ON TEMPORARY LICENCE (ROTL)

Release on Temporary Licence means being able to leave the prison for a short time. It is usually called ROTL for short.

You may get ROTL for the following things:

- To take part in paid or unpaid work
- To see children for whom you were the sole carer before you entered prison
- Because a family member is seriously ill
- To help you settle back into the community before you are released
- Not everyone gets or is eligible to be considered for ROTL, see below for more information about this.

If you are eligible it does not mean that you will be given ROTL – this will depend upon whether the prison thinks it is appropriate based on your sentence plan and any risks assessments that are carried out which will also look at your behaviour whilst in prison.

Some people cannot get ROTL. If you are any of the following you will NOT be able to get any type of ROTL:

- Category A or restricted status prisoner
- On the escape list
- Subject to extradition proceedings
- On remand or unsentenced
- Sentenced but remanded for further charges or further sentencing

- Held on some other matter or subject to possible immigration matters

You may be eligible to Restricted ROTL if you are:

- an indeterminate sentence prisoner (ISP);
- serving an Extended Determinate Sentence, or other legacy extended sentence;
- serving a sentence imposed under section 236A of the Criminal justice Act 2003 (offenders of particular concern)
- Assessed as high or very high risk of serious harm

If you fall into one of these categories you will have extra restrictions placed on ROTL which can include:

- You will need to be in an open prison to get ROTL (or assessed as suitable for open conditions for women).
- Your ROTL board must be chaired by a senior manager
- Your offender manager and police must be consulted about potential ROTL
- You will be subject to a higher level of monitoring whilst on release
- You may also be considered for Enhanced Behaviour Monitoring

If you are eligible for ROTL but do not fit into the above categories, you are subject to Standard ROTL.

There are many potential variations of ROTL so the specific options available to you are best discussed within the prison with your offender manager.

RELEASE DAY

The day has finally arrived, the day you're being released from prison, the day you can return to your loved ones and friends, breathe free air, eat what you like when you like and generally do all the legal things that you weren't able to do whilst you were in prison.

Now, you've probably known this day was coming but sometimes people get caught by surprise, maybe a recalculation of the release date by the staff in the OMU, maybe an appeal is granted, a court case is dropped, etc.

First of all, in English prisons nobody gets released at the weekend or on a public (bank) holiday; this means that if your release date falls on such a date then you'll be released the earliest working day before so if you're due to be released on a Saturday or a Sunday it will become a Friday release and if your release date falls on Easter Monday then you'll actually be released on the Thursday before Good Friday!

On the morning of your release you'll usually be informed by an officer fairly early on to pack your stuff (depending on what you may want to keep) and to get ready for release. Usually within a couple of hours (depending on the prison you're in and their daily routine) you'll be collected from your residential unit and escorted to Reception. Here you'll be reunited with most of your property that was being held that you weren't allowed in possession. You'll then be dealt with by either a Custodial Manager or Governor who will (should) go through the conditions of your licence, advise you of the requirement to attend an appointment with your probation officer usually the same day or the following day.

You will be given any money that you have saved or earned while you were in prison (the amount left in your spends or savings account. The prison may give you a travel warrant when leaving prison which will pay for your travel back home by bus / train. Most people will also get a discharge grant when released from prison that is a small amount of money which can help with immediate living expenses.

Some people will not be given a discharge grant. You will not get one if you are:

- under 18,
- serving a custodial sentence of 14 days or less,
- being transferred to a hospital under the Mental Health Act, or
- travelling to an address outside the United Kingdom.

You will also at this time be given back any other items that you arrived at the prison with such as mobile phones, jewellery, keys etc.

You will then be escorted by an officer to the main gate of the prison (this may not happen straight away as you may have to wait in a holding area for other prisoners to be processed) where some final checks will be carried out to confirm your identity before you are released from the prison.

Some people have family members waiting for them, personally I wouldn't recommend it as it's a very emotional day for all concerned and as you realistically can't tell anyone if you'll be out at 8am or 11am it can involve a lot of hanging around for people which can, oddly enough, lead to some stupid arguements about people being kept waiting, even though it wasn't in your control.

Most prisons have some form of public transport located fairly close by and I would suggest that as you'll probably have to attend a probation office appointment the same day it's possibly more sensible to make your way home after the probation meeting rather than having people hanging around twice during the day. However, it's your choice!

WORKING AFTER PRISON

Finding work after prison will probably be more difficult than it was before due to the fact that many employers will ask if you have a criminal record and you are under law obligated to be honest in your reply. Add to that the fact that your probation officer will probably want to contact your employer / visit you at your place of work and it's really not an option to hide your record.

Hopefully while in prison you managed to either attend some education or work classes that have improved your employability or given you the skills to consider becoming self-employed.

Speaking honestly, the only thing I can pretty much guarantee is that if you reoffend whilst on licence / parole the odds are highly stacked that you'll be returned to prison immediately and if convicted of a new offence your sentence will most likely be longer than your original one. I've seen people start out on 3 month sentences, get released, come back with a 12 month, released and back on 3 years, released and then back on a 5 or 10 year sentence.

If you discover it's too difficult finding legitimate employment now with a criminal record then maybe it's time you looked at becoming self-employed, maybe starting that small business you always thought about doing.

CONCLUSION

When writing this book I knew that there would typically be three types of readers, people who are potentially about to go into prison for the first time, the friends or relatives of people serving time in prison and those generally interested in British prisons and wanted to know the truth beyond the media headlines and recent TV programmes.

I'm going to repeat a statistic from the beginning of this book as I think it's necessary to keep things in perspective:

"70% of custodial sentences are imposed on those with at least seven previous convictions or cautions, and 50% are imposed on those with at least 15 previous convictions or cautions."

Most prisoners end up in prison after numerous run-ins with the police and the courts. To be sent to prison for a first offence is normally an indication of the seriousness or harm involved.

Prison is not an easy option, it is not a holiday camp but it also is not 'hard labour'.

British prisons are supposed to keep society safe by securely holding prisoners which on the whole they do an excellent job of.

Prison officers and other staff are tasked with keeping prisoners in a secure, safe environment and helping prisoners to rehabilitate to prevent their return to prison. Unfortunately the rehabilitation part of that equation relies not on the staff but the prisoners and there are many reasons why so many prisoners return to prison again and again, most of those reasons outside the realistic control of the staff in prisons.

Prison officers try to keep prisoners safe by enforcing the rules, the vast majority of officers are not on a power trip or deliberately annoying you and thankfully the days of officers being occasionally likely to dispense some physical punishment are long gone. Officers will treat you with respect if you do the same and try to remember that they didn't commit a crime, get convicted by a court, nor did they sentence you and they do not judge you.

A drug dealer earning thousands per day / week and able to afford all the trappings of wealth (cars, jewellery) and the side benefits of respect and glamourous companions is sadly unlikely to take a job in a shop, in McDonalds or even train as a plasterer upon their release; the difference in money and lifestyle is too great.

Once you take into account the fact that most people return to the same community, friends and associates that they were involved in previously and the likelihood of reoffending increases again.

In my experience, both as a person born and raised in England and as someone who's worked in multiple prisons in multiple roles and dealt with tens of thousands of prisoners over the years it's my belief that sadly some people are beyond saving.

For others, I'm glad to say the first time in prison will be their last, irrespective of the staff or the courses, but simply because of one of three things:

- The experience was such a shock to their system that they'll never come back
- Their offence that led to them being imprisoned was a one-off, not to be repeated
- They learnt from their mistake and won't be caught in the future

The best advice I can give anybody is "Don't come to prison" and whilst very few plan on coming to prison the unspoken part of that advice is "Don't do anything that could result in you being sent to prison".

If you've either enjoyed or found this book interesting then please do leave a review on Amazon as I do read every review and I like to know what my readers think.

Thank you.

Printed in Great Britain
by Amazon

21630053R00089